Know your furniture parts.

Here's how it all comes together.

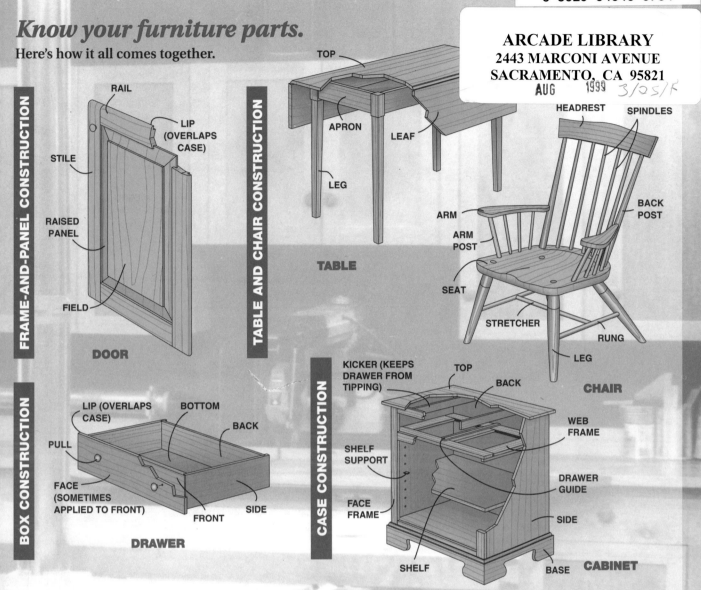

FRAME-AND-PANEL CONSTRUCTION

RAIL
LIP (OVERLAPS CASE)
STILE
RAISED PANEL
FIELD

DOOR

TABLE AND CHAIR CONSTRUCTION

TOP
APRON
LEAF
LEG

TABLE

HEADREST
SPINDLES
BACK POST
ARM
ARM POST
SEAT
STRETCHER
RUNG
LEG

CHAIR

BOX CONSTRUCTION

LIP (OVERLAPS CASE)
BOTTOM
BACK
PULL
FACE (SOMETIMES APPLIED TO FRONT)
FRONT
SIDE

DRAWER

CASE CONSTRUCTION

KICKER (KEEPS DRAWER FROM TIPPING)
TOP
BACK
WEB FRAME
SHELF SUPPORT
DRAWER GUIDE
FACE FRAME
SIDE
SHELF
BASE

CABINET

Know your decorative shapes.

These are the elements of woodworking style.

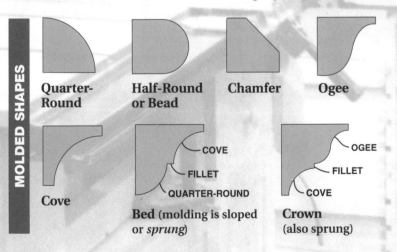

MOLDED SHAPES

Quarter-Round

Half-Round or Bead

Chamfer

Ogee

Cove

COVE
FILLET
QUARTER-ROUND

Bed (molding is sloped or *sprung*)

OGEE
FILLET
COVE

Crown (also sprung)

LEG SHAPES

POST
KNEE

KLE
OOT

Straight   Tapered   Cabriole

Secrets of Successful Woodworking™

Making Handsome Bookcases and Desks

SECRETS OF SUCCESSFUL WOODWORKING™

MAKING HANDSOME BOOKCASES AND DESKS

Nick Engler

Rodale Press, Inc.
Emmaus, Pennsylvania

OUR PURPOSE

*"We inspire and enable people to improve
their lives and the world around them."*

© 1999 by Bookworks, Inc.
Published by Rodale Press, Inc.
By arrangement with Bookworks, Inc.

The author and editors who compiled this book have tried
to make all of the contents as accurate and as correct as
possible. Plans, illustrations, photographs, and text have
all been carefully checked and cross-checked. However,
due to the variability of local conditions, construction
materials, personal skill, and so on, neither the author nor
Rodale Press assumes any responsibility for any injuries
suffered or for damages or other losses incurred that result
from the material presented herein. All instructions and
plans should be carefully studied and clearly understood
before beginning construction.

Printed in the United States of America on acid-free ∞,
recycled ♻ paper

**The Library of Congress has cataloged Volume 1
as follows:**

Engler, Nick.
    Making flawless cabinets and built-ins / Nick Engler.
        p.   cm.   (Secrets of successful
    woodworking ; #1)
    Includes bibliographical references and index.
    ISBN 0–87596–805–8   (Vol. 1 hardcover)
    1. Woodwork.   2. Cabinetwork.   3. Built-in
furniture.   I. Title.   II. Series: Engler, Nick. Secrets of
successful woodworking ; #1.
    TT180.E645   1998
    684.1'6—ddc21   98–8912

Vol. 3 ISBN 0–87596–819–8

Distributed in the book trade by St. Martin's Press

2 4 6 8 10 9 7 5 3 1   hardcover

Bookworks Staff
Designer: Linda Watts
Illustrator and Project Designer: Mary Jane Favorite
Interior and Back Cover Photographer: Karen Callahan
Master Craftsman: Jim McCann
Indexer: Beverly Bremer
Chief Executive Officer: Robert C. Sammons

Rodale Press Home and Garden Books Staff
Vice President and Editorial Director: Margaret J. Lydic
Managing Editor, Woodworking Books: Rick Peters
Editor: Tony O'Malley
Director of Design and Production: Michael Ward
Associate Art Director: Carol Angstadt
Cover Designer and design assistance: Dale Mack
Front Cover Photographer: Mitch Mandel
Studio Manager: Leslie M. Keefe
Copy Director: Dolores Plikaitis
Manufacturing Manager: Mark Krahforst
Manufacturing Coordinator: Patrick T. Smith
Office Manager: Karen Earl-Braymer

Special Thanks to:
Mr. and Mrs. David Roberts
Cincinnati, Ohio

Robertson's Cabinets
West Milton, Ohio

Troy-Hayner Cultural Center
Troy, Ohio

Wertz Stores
West Milton, Ohio

Workshops of David T. Smith
Morrow, Ohio

We're always happy to hear from you. For questions or
comments concerning the editorial content of this book,
please write to:
    Rodale Press, Inc.
    Book Readers' Service
    33 East Minor Street
    Emmaus, PA 18098

Look for other Rodale books wherever books are sold. Or
call us at (800) 848-4735.

For more information about Rodale Press and the books
and magazines we publish, visit our World Wide Web
site at:
    http://www.rodalepress.com

Customizing Your Home Office

There are few woodworking projects more personal than a desk. At its heart, it's nothing more than a chest of drawers with a work surface. But this is where you plan and pay for much of your life, write and talk to friends and relatives, and if you have a computer, reach out and explore your world. Bookcases are in the same boat. No two people on this planet have the same collection of books and other personal items that they want to display. Consequently, the style, size, and configuration of desks and bookcases are frequently tailored to their owners.

I've written this book to help you create truly personal furniture for your home office, helping to make it a more comfortable and enjoyable place in which to work. This is not just a *techniques* book, although it explains all the major construction methods needed to build bookcases and desks. And it's not just a *project* book, although there are complete plans and instructions for building ten different pieces of furniture. It's not just an *idea* book, although you'll find photographs of many different styles of desks and bookcases built by craftsmen all over this continent. It's not just a *jigs and fixtures* book, although you'll find plenty of them. It's *all of these* — and something completely different.

What you have here is a blow-by-blow description of what it took for a band of craftsmen to build the office furniture projects shown here — not just what we did, but also the problems that came up and how we solved them.

Making Handsome Bookcases and Desks starts out with a simple shelving project, the **Ropework Bookcase.** This shows you how to assemble a set of adjustable shelves, then enclose the case with a glazed door. With the **Built-In Bookcase,** we build and install a set of cabinets, making a floor-to-ceiling storage system. The **Rolltop Desk** is actually three projects in one. The "pedestals" that support the work surface are chests of drawers. Make one and you have a *filing cabinet.* Make two, add a work surface, and suspend a drawer between them, and you have a *pedestal desk.* Finally, add a set of pigeonholes on top of the work surface and enclose them with a tamboured door to make a

rolltop desk. The **Portable Desk** explores ways to take your paperwork with you. Finally, the **Computer Secretary** shows you a simple, ingenious way to integrate a computer workstation with a traditional desk design.

Now and then, I leave the story (briefly) to show you a *Quick Fixture* that will help speed up an operation or improve its accuracy. Or, to impart some useful *Shop Savvy* or *Methods of Work.* For example:

■ A **drilling guide** locates holes for adjustable shelving supports with no need for time-consuming measuring and layout.

■ **Corner squares** help you glue up perfectly square cases and drawers.

■ A **tambour assembly jig** holds dozens of thin tambours perfectly straight and square while you assemble them in a flexible door.

■ A **tenoning jig** supports large panels on their edge or end as you saw them to make raised panels or edge joinery.

I also show you how to straighten a board to make true rails and stiles, how to make half-blind dovetail joints in drawers, even how to arrange the components of a computer workstation.

And throughout, the *Look Here!* boxes help you navigate the book and find the information you need. For example, there's no sense in explaining how to make half-blind dovetails over and over again, so I invite you to *Look Here!* in the one place in the book where I do explain it every time I feel the knowledge might be helpful.

I've done it this way to help you build the desks and bookcases you want. You don't have to follow my play-by-play description of how to make a rolltop desk; you can adjust the size, style, or even mix and match features. Turn one of the pedestals into a computer cabinet, if that suits you. Or eliminate the moldings around the pedestal to give a traditional piece a contemporary look.

Building your own desks and bookcases opens up a world of possibilities; this book helps you take advantage of all of them.

With all good wishes,

Nick

Contents

ROPEWORK BOOKCASE   **2**

What size should it be?   3

Hanging, Standing, or Built In?   3

Standard Bookcase Dimensions   4

Design Savvy:
Shelving Construction   6

What style will it be?   7

Design Savvy:
The Millennium Style   9

Materials List   10

How do I build it?   11

Selecting and Preparing the Stock   11

Shop Savvy:
Truing a Board   11

Making the Case   13

Quick Fixture:
Self-Clamping Guide   14

Quick Fixture:
Drilling Guide   15

Finishing Up   19

Alternatives:
Door Frame Joinery   20

A Bonus Project:
BOOK SLIP   **22**

Materials List   23

BUILT-IN BOOKCASE   **24**

What size should it be?   25

Standard Dimensions for Built-In Units   26

Design Savvy:
Making a Built-In Turn a Corner   26

What style will it be?   27

Materials List   28

How do I build it?   30

Preparing the Materials   30

Shop Savvy:
Double-Cutting Sheet Materials   30

Building the Base Unit   31

No Problem:
Squaring a Case   33

Quick Fixture:
Corner Squares   33

Alternatives:
Cupboard Doors   34

Methods of Work:
Making a Lock Joint   36

Building the Top Unit   37

Methods of Work:
Making a Dowel Joint   38

Alternatives:
Adjustable Shelving Supports   38

Installing the Units   39

No Problem:
Re-routing Heating Vents   40

Methods of Work:
Installing Corner Molding   41

A Bonus Project:
INSET SHELVES   **42**

Materials List   42

Making the Shelving Unit   43

Installing the Unit   43

A Bonus Project:
QUICK-AND-EASY SHELVES   **44**

Materials List   45

Making the Parts   46

Assembling the Shelves   46

ROLLTOP DESK   **48**

What size should it be?   49

What style will it be?   51

Design Savvy:
Desk Construction   52

Materials List: Pedestal/Filing Cabinet   56

How do I build it?   57

Building the Pedestals   57

Another Way to Go:
  Frame-and-Panel Construction   57

Methods of Work:
  Routing Half-Blind Dovetails   62

Another Way to Go:
  Drawer Guides   63

Design Savvy:
  Cabinets for Computers   64

Materials List: Desktop and Drawer   66

Making a Pedestal Desk   67

Another Way to Go:
  Drawer Brackets   70

Quick Fixture:
  Extension Slide Drill Guide   71

Materials List: Rolltop and Pigeonholes   72

Making the Rolltop   73

Shop Savvy:
  Laying Out an Oval   73

Shop Savvy:
  Designing and Assembling
  Tamboured Doors   78

Quick Fixture:
  Tambour Assembly Jig   79

Methods of Work:
  Making Lock Joints   82

PORTABLE DESK   84

What size should it be?   85

What style will it be?   86

Materials List   88

How do I build it?   89

Preparing the Stock   89

Methods of Work:
  Joining Breadboard Ends   89

Making the Joinery   91

Quick Fixture:
  Finger Joint Jig   92

Methods of Work:
  Making Finger Joints   93

Making the Legs   94

Assembling the Desk   95

COMPUTER SECRETARY   96

What size should it be?   97

What style will it be?   98

Materials List   100

How do I build it?   103

Preparing the Materials   103

Making the Cases   103

Making the Doors   108

Methods of Work:
  Joining Door Frames with Decorative Edges   110

Quick Fixture:
  Frame-and-Panel Construction Aids   111

Methods of Work:
  Driving Square Pegs in Round Holes   112

Making the Pigeonholes   113

Making the Drawers and Shelves   114

Finishing the Desk   115

For Your Shop: A Bonus Project: WORKSHOP SECRETARY   116

Materials List   117

How do I build it?   118

Preparing the Stock   118

Cutting the Joinery   118

Drilling the Support Holes   120

Assembling the Cabinets   120

Hanging the Secretary   121

INDEX   122

Ropework
Bookcase

In this chapter...

PRACTICAL KNOW-HOW

Standard Bookcase Dimensions	4
Shelving Construction	6
Making the Case	13
Making the Door Frames	17
Door Frame Joinery	20

JIGS AND FIXTURES

Self-Clamping Guide	14
Drilling Guide	15

SHOP SOLUTIONS

Truing a Board	11

A bookcase is a wonderfully simple piece of furniture. At its heart, it's nothing more than a box with doors that open to the front. Everything else is just window dressing.

The window dressing on this particular bookcase — the "ropework" muntins — grew out of a conversation I had with Jim McCann, the master craftsman I work with. "We need to start the book out with a simple bookcase," I told him. "Something that shows all the basics — case, shelves, glazed doors." Jim gave me a been-there-done-that look he reserves for those occasions when I bring him a project idea that's just too boring for words. "Okay," I replied, "what can we do that's new and fun, shows all the basics, and is easy to build?"

The best place to start when you're searching for a new design is to review what's been done before. Jim and I got out our furniture books and looked through them for inspiration. Several cabinets from Greene and Greene caught our eye. The Greenes were California craftsmen who built their own distinctive style of Arts and Crafts furniture during the first part of the twentieth century. Some of the muntins in their doors, I noticed, weren't perfectly straight. They had a dogleg in the middle. I sketched

a bookcase with several horizontal dogleg muntins in the doors. Jim studied it a moment, then added a vertical muntin with doglegs where it crossed the horizontal muntins. "Looks like knotted rope," Jim commented. Then he got busy.

What size should it be?

There's more that goes into designing a bookcase than that, of course. The first thing you need to decide is how big to make it. That depends on not only how many books you have but also whether you want it to hold other objects (like stereo equipment and rock collections), who will use it, and whether it will hang, stand, or be built in.

HANGING, STANDING, OR BUILT IN?

A "standing" bookcase rests on the floor. The weight of the books is transferred from the shelves to the side supports and directly to the floor. Consequently, standing cases can be quite large — some reach nearly to the ceiling.

A hanging bookcase is attached to a wall, secured to studs or masonry. In these cases, the weight is transferred from the shelves to the sides and to a "nailing strip" at the back of the case, just under the top. The nailing strip is bolted to the wall. Hanging bookcases are typically smaller than standing cases for the simple reason that they don't reach all the way to the floor.

Standing bookcases rest on the floor. All the weight is supported by the sides.

Hanging bookcases are attached to a wall. All the weight is supported by a nailing strip near the top of the case. Extremely heavy hanging cases may have two nailing strips — one just under the top and the other under the bottom shelf.

A built-in bookcase may be small or large — it's typically customized to fit the space that you have to fill. Large built-in cases are made up of smaller units, both hanging and standing. This makes them easier to install. The units are attached to each other and to the wall.

WHO WILL USE IT? The level of the shelves in a bookcase depends on who will use the bookcase. Men, women, teens, and children all have different body sizes; consequently, their "reach" differs. You must plan the shelving levels so the person using the case can easily see and reach the objects on the shelves. For example, the maximum reach for the average man is 83 inches; for an average woman, 77 inches. Consequently, the maximum shelving height that most furniture designers use for bookcases is somewhat below the average reach for both men and women — 72 inches.

SHELVING SPAN AND DEPTH The span (side-to-side dimension) of a shelf depends on the material of which it's made and the weight of materials resting on it. (Books weigh no more than 20 to 25 pounds per foot, usually.) If the shelf is too long for the weight, it will sag. Solid wood will support the

A large *built-in bookcase* is made up of several smaller units. Because these units are attached to each other and to the wall, the structure doesn't have to be as substantial as it is for a stand-alone bookcase. The structure of the house will help support the weight.

DESIGN SAVVY

If your bookcase incorporates drawers, the top edge of the highest drawer should be no more than 55 inches above the floor. Higher than that and the average adult won't be able to see the contents.

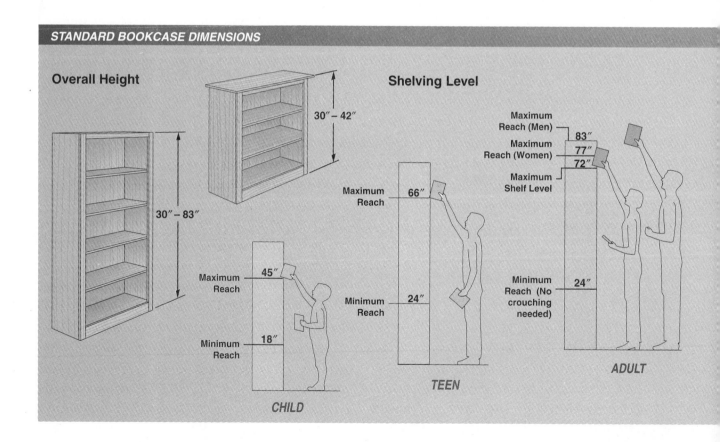

STANDARD BOOKCASE DIMENSIONS

Overall Height

30″ – 42″

30″ – 83″

Shelving Level

Maximum Reach (Men) — 83″
Maximum Reach (Women) — 77″
72″
Maximum Shelf Level

Maximum Reach — 66″

Maximum Reach — 45″

Minimum Reach — 24″

Minimum Reach (No crouching needed) — 24″

Minimum Reach — 18″

CHILD

TEEN

ADULT

most weight and allows for the longest spans, followed by plywood and particleboard, in that order. If you need to build a case wider than the allowable span, incorporate one or more vertical *dividers* in the bookcase. Dividers reduce the span of the shelves without sacrificing much storing space.

The objects resting on the shelves determine the depth (front-to-back dimension). The standard depth for bookshelves is 10 to 12 inches, but if you want to store audio components with the books, the shelves will have to be at least 18 inches deep.

SHELF SPACING The distance between the shelves is also determined by what they hold, but a set of shelves looks best when you arrange them so the larger spaces are toward the bottom and the smaller ones toward the top. In a well-designed bookcase, shelves are often spaced according to a simple mathematical progression. Of course, spacing is not an issue for bookcases with adjustable shelves.

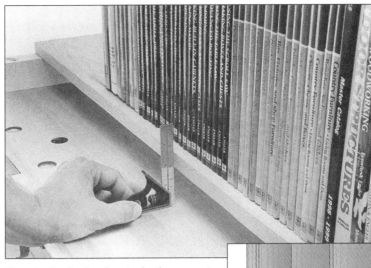

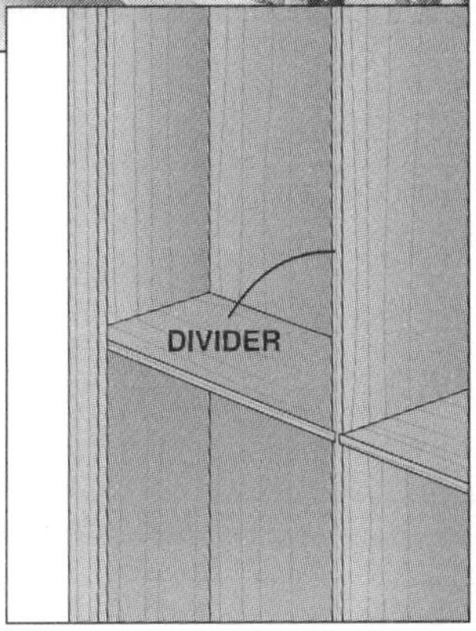

If you're in doubt about whether or not a shelving material will sag at a given span, cut a sample shelf from the material. Rest it on two blocks — the distance between the blocks must equal the span. Measure the height of the shelf above the workbench, then place a typical load on the shelf and measure again. If the shelf sags more than $1/32$ to $1/16$ inch, use a stronger material, reduce the span, or add a divider to the case.

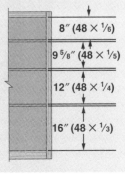

DIVIDER

Depth of Shelves

Small or narrow objects	6"–8"
Books or large objects	10"–12"
Audio components	18"–20"
Video components	18"–24"
Computer components	15"–18"

Shelving Span

(Maximum span for a 12-inch-wide shelf supporting 25 pounds per running foot)

³⁄₄"-thick particleboard	24"
³⁄₄"-thick plywood	30"
³⁄₄"-thick softwood	36"
³⁄₄"-thick hardwood	48"
1"-thick softwood	48"
1"-thick hardwood	54"
1½"-thick softwood	66"
1½"-thick hardwood	78"

Shelf Spacing

Arithmetic Progression
The spacing between each successive shelf is a constant amount larger than the space above it. The sequence 8, 10, and 12 builds on a constant of 2.

8"
10" (8 + 2)
12" (10 + 2)
14" (12 + 2)

Geometric Progression
The spacing between shelves builds on a constant ratio. For example, the numbers 8, 10, and 12½ build on a ratio of 1.25. Each number is 1.25 times the preceding number.

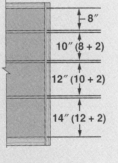

8"
10" (8 × 1.25)
12½" (10 × 1.25)
15 ⅝" (12½ × 1.25)

Harmonic Progression
The spacing ratios are reciprocals of a sequence. You obtain a reciprocal by dividing a number into 1. The sequence 1/3, 1/4, 1/5, 1/6 is the harmonic of 3, 4, 5, 6.

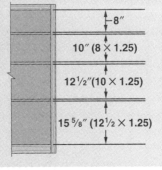

8" (48 × ⅙)
9 ⅝" (48 × ⅕)
12" (48 × ¼)
16" (48 × ⅓)

DESIGN SAVVY ■ *Shelving Construction*

To most people, a *bookcase* is any type of shelving unit that holds books. As a craftsman, you may want to be more specific.

There are four common types of shelving, each one constructed slightly differently from the others.

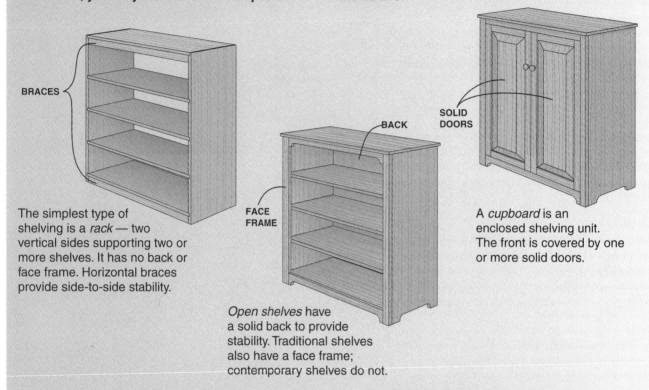

The simplest type of shelving is a *rack* — two vertical sides supporting two or more shelves. It has no back or face frame. Horizontal braces provide side-to-side stability.

Open shelves have a solid back to provide stability. Traditional shelves also have a face frame; contemporary shelves do not.

A *cupboard* is an enclosed shelving unit. The front is covered by one or more solid doors.

A *display case* is what many people think of when you mention a bookcase. This is built much like a cupboard with one exception. The doors are either made of glass or they are *glazed* (wooden frames with glass panes). This allows you to see the contents of the case. Yet the case is completely enclosed to protect the items stored in it.

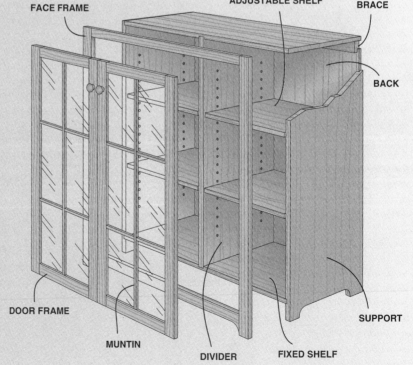

What style will it be?

The Ropework Bookcase was inspired by an Arts and Crafts design, then evolved to what has come to be known as a "Studio" design. The term encompasses a multitude of highly individual designs that are built by craftsmen today. If this design doesn't suit your fancy, no problem. It's an easy matter to change the style of a bookcase simply by altering the design of the moldings, muntins, and other decorative elements.

Courtesy of the Hayner Cultural Center, Troy, OH.

FEDERAL STYLE

Bookcases were uncommon before the Civil War because it was rare to find a person who owned enough books to require a case for them. Private libraries tended to be small, and the bookcases were incorporated into a desk or a cabinet. Such is the case with this Federal breakfront from the early days of the nineteenth century. This type of construction was sometimes called "case over case" — in this instance, a display case over a cupboard.

COUNTRY STYLE

Country designs are simplified versions of classic pieces — Queen Anne, Chippendale, and Federal. Country designs were made for clientele who could not afford high style. There are many examples of simple Country shelving units, such as the "whale-end" rack *(above, left)*, but few true bookcases. Most are pieces that were converted later when books became more affordable. The case shown at the left was an old pie safe until it was altered to hold books.

GOLDEN OAK STYLE

Toward the end of the nineteenth century, new printing technologies made books less expensive and middle-class folks began to collect personal libraries. The new furniture industry jumped to fill the demand and began to turn out bookcases of all sizes. Most of these were late Victorian designs, simplified for mass production. Manufacturers preferred to use oak for these pieces because the wood machined well and stood up to the rigors of shipping. Consequently, these designs became known collectively as the "Golden Oak" or "Victorian Oak" style. The stacking "barrister" bookcase shown at left consists of several boxes stacked one on top of the other. This design allowed customers to purchase as many shelves as they needed.

MISSION STYLE

The Arts and Crafts movement was a reaction against mass-produced Victorian designs. Its proponents emphasized simplicity, utility, and "honest craftsmanship." Arts and Crafts furniture — commonly called "Mission" furniture — often used visible joinery (called *frank* joinery) as decorative as well as structural elements. For example, the pegs and the ends of the tenons are visible in this piece to add visual interest to an otherwise austere design.

DESIGN SAVVY ■ *The Millennium Style*

The appearance of a distinct new furniture style is a rare event, but that's just what's happening as we turn a new millennium. Nicknamed the *Millennium* style, these designs have evolved from Postmodern furniture. Postmodern designs began to appear in the 1970s as craftsmen rebelled against the dearth of ornament in the then-popular Contemporary and Modern styles. Furniture makers began to mix modern furniture forms with classical design elements, producing a contemporary style with a traditional touch. The Millennium style carries this a step further, blending contemporary designs with older "utilitarian" styles, particularly Shaker and Mission, to create a unique look.

Courtesy of M.T. Maxwell Furniture Company, Bedford, VA.

Courtesy of Kevin Kopil Furniture Design, Jonesville, VT. Photo by Stayner & Stayner.

Courtesy of M.T. Maxwell Furniture Company, Bedford, VA.

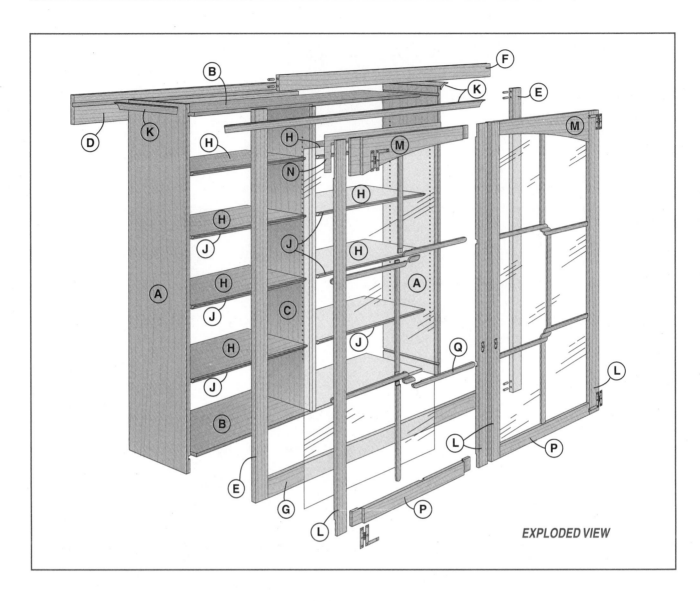

EXPLODED VIEW

ROPEWORK BOOKCASE ■ MATERIALS LIST *(Finished Dimensions)*

PARTS

A	Sides* (2)	¾″ × 11½″ × 65″
B	Top/bottom* (2)	¾″ × 11½″ × 47¼″
C	Divider*	¾″ × 11½″ × 60½″
D	Nailing strip	¾″ × 6″ × 46½″
E	Face frame stiles (2)	¾″ × 2″ × 65″
F	Top face frame rail	¾″ × 2¾″ × 44″
G	Bottom face frame rail	¾″ × 3″ × 44″
H	Adjustable shelves* (8)	¾″ × 10¾″ × 22¾″
J	Banding (total)	¾″ × ¾″ × 245″
K	Cove molding (total)	¾″ × 2⅝″ × 82″
L	Door stiles (4)	¾″ × 1¾″ × 59¼″
M	Top door rails (2)	⅝″ × 6″ × 21⅝″

N	Top door rail backs (2)	⅛″ × 6″ × 21⅝″
P	Bottom door rails (2)	¾″ × 2½″ × 21⅝″
Q	Muntin strips (total)	⅜″ × ¾″ × 192″

Make these parts from plywood.

HARDWARE

H-L hinges and mounting screws (2 sets, top and bottom)

Surface-mounted cabinet locks and mounting screws (2)

Lock escutcheons (2)

#8 × 1″ Flathead wood screws (11)

⅛″ × 18⅞″ × 55½″ Glass panes (2)

Shelf support pins (32)

How do I build it?

When building a piece of case furniture, the rule of thumb that I have tattooed to the back of my eyelids is:

- Begin with the case
- Then fill up the openings
- And add the decorations

That served Jim and me well here. We began by assembling the case. Then we made the doors to fit the openings and added the decorative cove molding.

SELECTING AND PREPARING THE STOCK

Before you can do anything, however, you must choose the materials for this project. Bookcases require an enormous amount of lumber, so we chose to make the case parts and shelves from cabinet-grade plywood. This saved both money and headaches — we didn't have to worry about the wide parts cupping. For the remaining parts — rails, stiles, moldings, and nailing strip — we used solid wood.

SHOP DRYING Jim brought *all* the stock — solid wood *and* plywood — into the shop to let it "shop dry" for a week or so before working with it. This allowed the moisture content in the materials a chance to reach equilibrium with the relative humidity in our shop. If you work a piece of lumber before it has a chance to shop dry, it may shrink or swell as it releases or absorbs moisture. It's always best to wait until the materials stabilize.

You may wonder why we shop dry plywood. After all, aren't sheet materials much more stable than solid wood? Yes, they are. But they *do* move, even though the movement is slight. Jim and I have had a few problems with sheet materials in motion, so we take no chances and shop dry *everything*.

After the lumber has shop dried, look it over and carefully decide which piece of wood you'll use to make what part. Bust the lumber down to manageable sizes, true the boards, and plane them to the thicknesses you need. Most of the parts in this project are ¾ inch thick, with the exception of the

SHOP SAVVY ■ *Truing a Board*

After the lumber has shop dried, measure and mark the parts of the project on the boards. As you do, leave extra stock, making the parts 1 to 2 inches longer than their final dimensions. Cut the lumber into small bolts, 2 to 6 feet long. You don't have to cut every part, just saw up the lumber into easily manageable sizes.

Craftsmen refer to this as *busting down* the lumber. Not only does it make the boards easier to handle, it helps relieve stresses in the wood. As a tree grows, it often buttresses itself against wind or gravity. These internal tensions remain until you release them by cutting the wood apart. As they are released, the wood may bow or warp slightly, but that's okay. Since you've cut the parts oversized, you have the extra stock needed to true them.

True the lumber with a jointer and a planer.

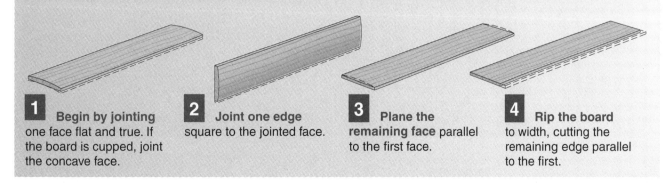

1 **Begin by jointing** one face flat and true. If the board is cupped, joint the concave face.

2 **Joint one edge** square to the jointed face.

3 **Plane the remaining face** parallel to the first face.

4 **Rip the board** to width, cutting the remaining edge parallel to the first.

top door rails and top door rail backs. These are ⅝ and ⅛ inch thick, respectively.

When selecting wood for the door rails and stiles, take special care to get straight grain. The stiles especially are long, slender pieces, and if the grain isn't perfectly straight, the parts may bow or warp even after you true them. Jim painstakingly inspected and trued all the lumber in our door frames, but he missed one little portion in an inside stile when the grain changed direction abruptly. As a result, the stile slowly bowed over the time that Jim took to build and fit the doors. When he went to hang the door, the bad stile was "sprung," protruding from the case about ¼ inch when the door closed.

At all costs, avoid *reaction wood* for frame members. All wood has some internal tension, but reaction wood is highly stressed. When you rip it, the board bends or bows perceptibly. In some cases, it may pinch the sides of the saw kerf

SHOP SAVVY

When choosing lumber that must remain true, inspect the quarter grain at the edge of the board, where the wood is cut roughly perpendicular to the annual rings. If the grain lines are relatively straight *(left)*, even though they may slope at an angle through the board, the wood will likely remain flat. If they have tight curves or change directions abruptly *(right)*, the board is more likely to bow or twist.

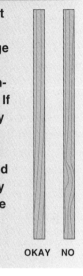

OKAY   NO

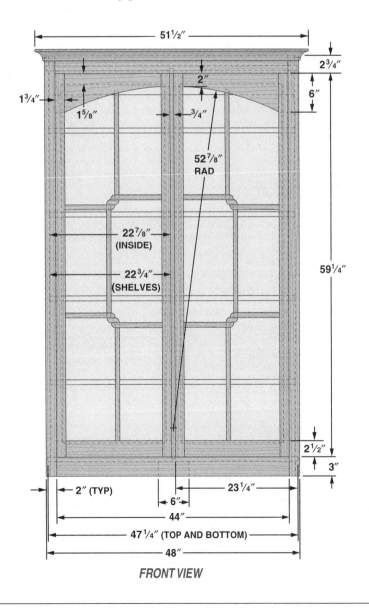

FRONT VIEW

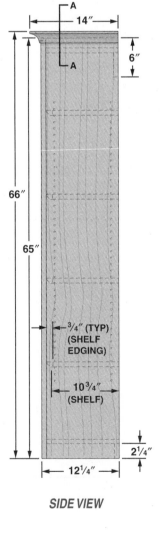

SIDE VIEW

together, causing the blade to bind. Reaction wood often continues to bend for days after it's cut, as the internal stresses slowly dissipate. It can be used for parts that will be assembled in such a way that the structure holds them straight, but door frames don't do this.

MAKING THE CASE

The case part of this bookcase is just a big box with a divider down the middle. All the plywood parts — sides, divider, top, bottom — are assembled with dadoes.

CUTTING THE JOINTS There are several tools you can use to create rabbets and dadoes, but when working with large pieces, I prefer a hand-held router. It's easier to move the router over the work than it is the other way around.

Lay out and rout the dadoes in the sides, top, and bottom. Note that these dadoes are labeled as ¾ inch wide and ⅜ inch deep on the drawings. If you're making the case from plywood, remember that a standard sheet is actually ¹⁄₃₂ inch thinner than its nominal thickness. Manufacturers offer special ²³⁄₃₂-inch straight bits just to rout dadoes for ¾-inch plywood.

After routing the dadoes, cut the notch in the divider for the nailing strip.

SHOP SAVVY

When selecting router bits for general work in solid wood, don't be swayed by manufacturers' claims of hardness. Any grade of carbide works well. However, if you do extensive work in plywood or particleboard, choose a C3 or C4 grade. Sheet materials are modestly abrasive, and the harder grades of carbide will wear longer.

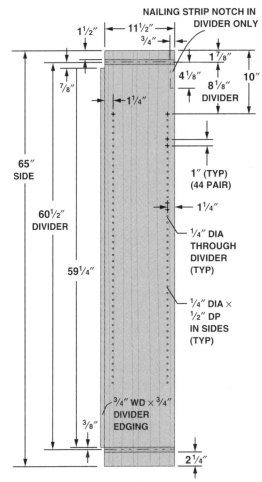

SIDE AND DIVIDER LAYOUT

When routing dadoes in long, wide boards such as the sides of a bookcase, make a long, straight guide for the router. This particular guide fits over a bar clamp so you can clamp it to the work.

To help position the guide accurately, attach an "indicator base" to one side. Make this base from a thin piece of plywood or hardboard. Clamp the guide to a scrap. With the router and the bit you will use to cut the joints, rout through the base *(left)*. To use the base as an indicator, align the edge with the mark that indicates the side of the dado you want to rout *(top right)*. Secure the guide to the work. The guide works equally well for routing rabbets *(bottom right)*.

QUICK FIXTURE ■ *Self-Clamping Guide*

A simple box that fits around a pipe clamp makes a great guide or an auxiliary fence. The sides of the box serve as straightedges, while the pipe clamp secures it to the work. The box is open at the bottom to give you quick access to the clamp jaws.

Select a clamp for ½-inch I.D. pipe. Plan the box so the inside dimension from end to end is the same as the length of the pipe. Cut the parts and drill ⅝-inch-diameter holes in the ends. Assemble the box with glue (don't use any metal fasteners), then joint the sides straight and true.

Cut two short lengths of ⅝-inch-diameter dowel. Taper one end of each dowel to fit the pipe like a plug. Assemble the clamp on the pipe, place the pipe inside the box, and drive the dowel plugs through the holes in the ends and into the pipe. Secure the dowel by driving flathead wood screws through the ends and into the sides of the dowels. Countersink the screws *below* the surface of the box so they won't scratch the work. Should you ever need to remove the clamp from the box, back out the screws and remove the dowels.

To use the guide, adjust the sliding jaw so the distance between the jaws is slightly more than the work. Secure the clamp, making sure the bottom edges of the box are flat on the work so the box doesn't rock.

The open bottom of the guide box lets you move the sliding jaw of the pipe clamp without interference.

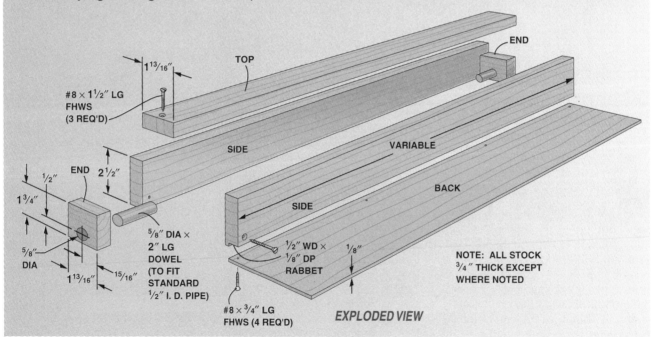

EXPLODED VIEW

TOP

END

SIDE

VARIABLE

BACK

SIDE

#8 × 1½″ LG FHWS (3 REQ'D)

1 13/16″

END   2½″

½″

1 ¾″

⅝″ DIA

1 13/16″   15/16″

⅝″ DIA × 2″ LG DOWEL (TO FIT STANDARD ½″ I.D. PIPE)

½″ WD × ⅛″ DP RABBET

⅛″

#8 × ¾″ LG FHWS (4 REQ'D)

NOTE: ALL STOCK ¾″ THICK EXCEPT WHERE NOTED

DRILLING THE SUPPORT HOLES The shelves in this bookcase are adjustable. They rest on movable pins, set in rows of holes. By moving the pins, you can move the shelves to whatever level you need.

This is a simple system, but it requires some precision. All four rows of holes — one at each corner of the shelves — must be precisely the same. If one row is off, all the shelves will be unstable. The easiest way I've found to make the rows precisely the same is to make a drilling guide and use it for all the rows. Even if the holes in the guide are off a little bit, it won't matter because all the rows you make with the guide will be off the same amount.

ASSEMBLING THE CASE Once you've cut the joinery and drilled the holes for shelving supports, assemble the basic case — sides, top, bottom, divider, and nailing strip. Glue together the sides, top, bottom, and divider. However, attach the nailing strip with glue *and* fasteners to the sides and divider. Jim fastened the center of the nailing strip to the divider with ordinary screws, then secured the ends to the sides with pocket screws. If you don't have a guide to drill screw pockets, you might use biscuits or dowels instead.

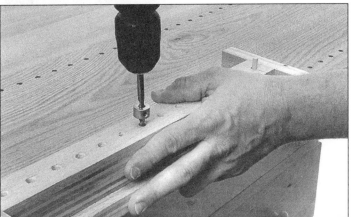

A drilling guide helps you to drill rows of holes all exactly the same. When drilling a row longer than the guide itself, index the guide by placing a dowel in the first guide hole, then inserting the other end of the dowel in the last hole drilled.

QUICK FIXTURE ■ *Drilling Guide*

A drilling guide eliminates a lot of layout work and makes it easy to locate holes accurately. To make the jig, glue two long scraps of ¾-inch plywood face to face. After the glue dries, trim the stock to size, mark the holes, and drill them. Then attach a bracket to each end. When you use the drilling guide, hook the brackets over the edge of the work.

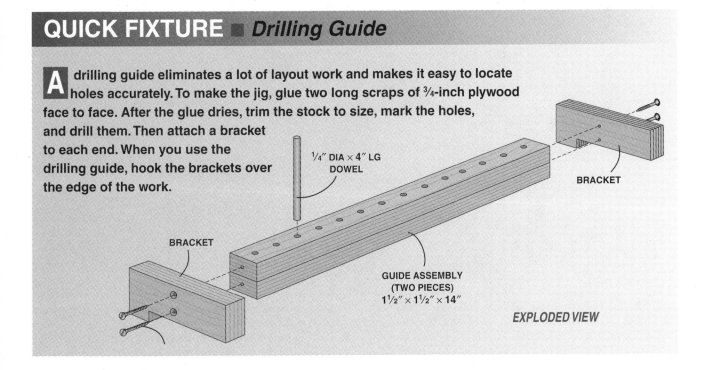

¼" DIA × 4" LG DOWEL

BRACKET

BRACKET

GUIDE ASSEMBLY
(TWO PIECES)
1½" × 1½" × 14"

EXPLODED VIEW

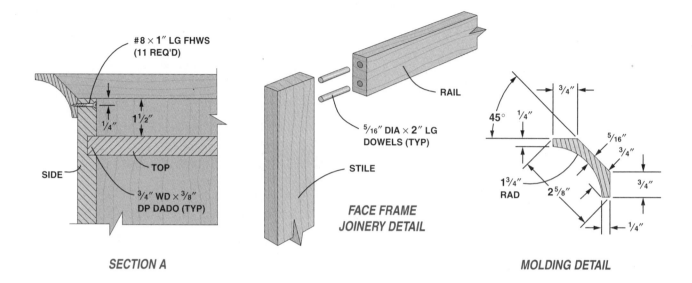

SECTION A

FACE FRAME JOINERY DETAIL

MOLDING DETAIL

(Section A labels) #8 × 1" LG FHWS (11 REQ'D); 1½"; ¼"; SIDE; TOP; ¾" WD × ⅜" DP DADO (TYP)

(Face Frame Joinery Detail labels) RAIL; 5/16" DIA × 2" LG DOWELS (TYP); STILE

(Molding Detail labels) 45°; ¼"; ¾"; 5/16"; ¾"; 1¾" RAD; 2⅝"; ¾"; ¼"

MAKING THE FACE FRAME The case is fitted with a face frame to hide the case joinery and strengthen the assembly. Jim joined the frame members with dowels, as shown in the *Face Frame Joinery Detail,* but you can also use biscuits, pocket screws, lap joints, or mortises and tenons. Assemble the frame, let the glue dry, then glue the frame to the front edges of the case.

ADDING THE COVE MOLDING The cove molding at the top of the bookcase is known as a *sprung* molding. It leans out from the case at an angle, making the piece seem to flare at the top. Cut the shape of the molding on a table saw, passing the stock across the blade at an angle to make the cove. Miter the adjoining pieces, then attach them to the top edges of the sides and face frame with glue and screws.

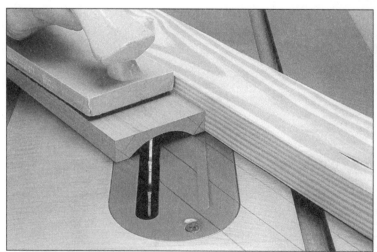

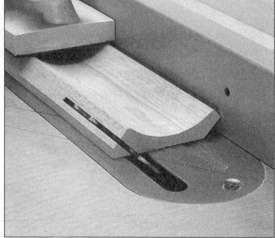

To create the cove molding, first cut a cove in the face of the stock by passing it across the blade at a 45 degree angle. Attach a straightedge to the worktable with double-faced carpet tape and guide the stock along it, cutting against the rotation of the blade. Make very shallow cuts, removing no more than 1/16 inch in a single pass, until the cove is ½ inch deep. Afterward, bevel the edges of the molding with the blade tilted to 45 degrees.

MAKING THE DOOR FRAMES The door rails and stiles are joined with lap joints at the corners, then the inside edges are rabbeted to hold the glass panes. That is, three of the four frame members are rabbeted. The fourth member — the top door rail — is built up from two parts, one ⅝ inch thick and the other ⅛ inch thick. The thinner part is cut in the shape of a long, inverted U. When glued to the thick part, it forms the top of the glass rabbet.

Jim decided to assemble the doors in this manner for several reasons. If he had simply cut a rabbet to follow the arch in the top rails, the glass pane would have to be specially cut, and this would have added to the expense. Routing a straight rabbet in a curved part requires a jig of some sort, and this would have added to the construction time. The method Jim chose saved time and money.

SHOP SAVVY

When making inset doors, I usually make them to the exact size of the opening, then plane them to fit. That way, if the opening is slightly out of square, I can still get a good fit.

Create the corner lap joints with a router or a dado cutter, cutting each lap ⅜ inch deep. After cutting the laps, lay out and cut the arches in the top rails. Drill half-round mortises in the edges of the stiles and rails to hold the muntin assemblies, as shown in the photo on page 18. Glue the frames together (including the ⅛-inch-thick rail back), let the glue dry, then rout the rabbets in the stiles and bottom rails. Where the router bit leaves a rounded corner, square it with a chisel.

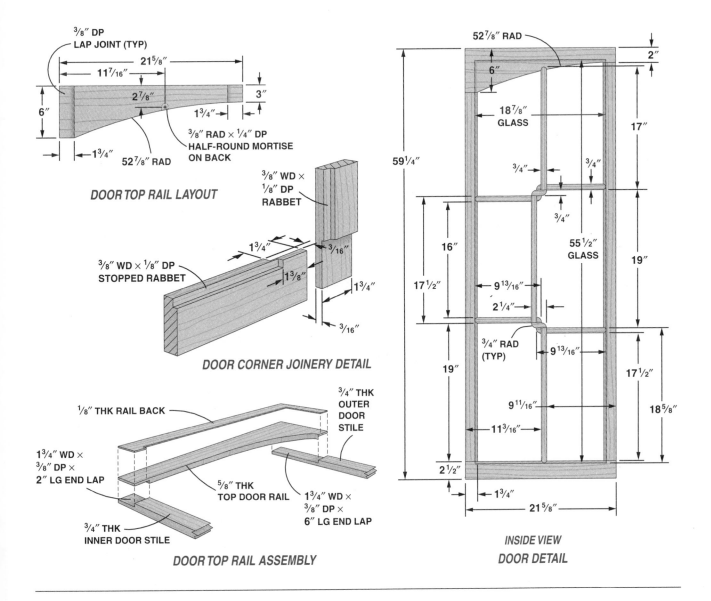

DOOR TOP RAIL LAYOUT

DOOR CORNER JOINERY DETAIL

DOOR TOP RAIL ASSEMBLY

**INSIDE VIEW
DOOR DETAIL**

INSTALLING THE MUNTINS The ropework muntins are strips of wood, slightly rounded at the arrises with sandpaper or a file. Like the door frames, they are joined with lap joints at the "knot." Cut crosslaps in the horizontal muntins and end laps in the vertical muntins, as shown in the *Knot Detail*.

Pay close attention to which surface you cut as you make each lap joint. The orientation of the laps affects the appearance of the knots. If the joints are facing the wrong way, they won't look like knots. Jim laid out all the muntins on the workbench before he cut them, arranged them as he planned to assemble them, then clearly marked the locations of the lap joints.

Round the muntin ends where shown in the *Knot Detail* and glue the laps together to make three assemblies for each door — two L-shaped assemblies (for the top and bottom of the door) and one U-shaped (for the middle). Join these assemblies edge to edge with a 2¼-inch-long muntin strip between each to form the knots. Finally, glue the ends of the muntins in the half-round mortises.

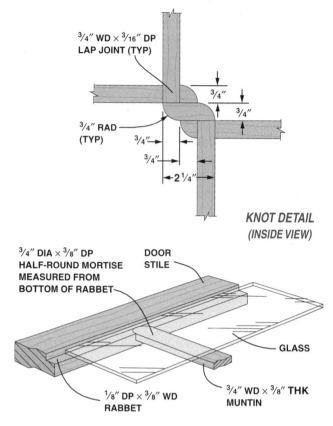

3/4" WD × 3/16" DP LAP JOINT (TYP)

3/4"

3/4"

3/4" RAD (TYP)

3/4"

3/4"

2¼"

KNOT DETAIL
(INSIDE VIEW)

3/4" DIA × 3/8" DP HALF-ROUND MORTISE MEASURED FROM BOTTOM OF RABBET

DOOR STILE

GLASS

1/8" DP × 3/8" WD RABBET

3/4" WD × 3/8" THK MUNTIN

DOOR STILE, MUNTIN, AND GLASS ASSEMBLY DETAIL

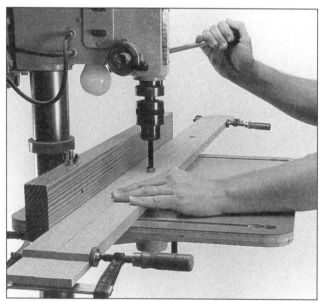

To make the half-round mortises that hold the muntins, clamp two rails or two stiles together, edge to edge. Using a Forstner bit, drill a shallow hole centered on the seam between the two boards. When you take the boards apart, there will be a mortise in each.

After assembling the muntins and installing them in the door frame, you may want to do a little detail work to make the knots look more like knots. Jim distinguished the individual "cords" in each knot by cutting shallow grooves with a V-gouge. Then he rounded the arrises slightly with sandpaper.

FINISHING UP

Once you've made the doors, most of the hard work is done. There are just a few odds and ends to take care of.

BANDING THE SHELVES Jim and I elected to make the adjustable shelves from plywood. Although hardwood is stronger, plywood offered sufficient strength for the short span of these shelves. If you use plywood, cover the front edges with a hardwood strip or *banding* to hide the plies.

No matter what material you use, bevel the front edges of the shelves as shown in the *Shelf Edge Detail*. The reason is aesthetic — if you leave the edges square, they will be visible as horizontal lines behind the glazed doors. This will detract from the visual effect of the ropework muntins. When the edges are beveled, they are less visible.

INSTALLING THE DOORS Fit the doors to the opening so there's about 1/16 inch of clearance all around each door. (Jim uses a dime as a gauge.) Using toothpicks or matchsticks, wedge the doors in place in their openings and install the H-L hinges. These hinges simply rest on top of the wood surface; there's no need to cut mortises for them. The horizontal arm on each hinge should straddle the seam between the rail and the stile. This reinforces the lap joints.

INSTALLING THE CABINET LOCKS The locks and keys serve as both door pulls and catches on this project. To install a lock, drill a keyhole in the stile. Attach the lock to the back face and the escutcheon to the front. When the door is closed and locked, the latch should rest in the slot near the front edge of the divider.

FINISHING Remove the doors, locks, and hinges. Set the hardware aside and finish sand the wood surfaces. Apply a finish to the bookcase and the doors.

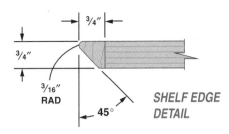

SHELF EDGE DETAIL

FINAL INSTALLATION Hang the case before replacing the doors and hardware. Secure the nailing strip to the studs in the wall with carriage bolts. When installing a shelving unit this size, I also attach a hardwood ledger strip to the wall for the bottom shelf to rest on. That way, you don't have all the weight hanging from a single strip. It also simplifies the installation. Attach the bottom strip to the wall first, rest the unit on it, then attach the nailing strip.

When the bookcase is installed, mount the glass in the doors. Replace the doors, hinges, and locks.

TRY THIS!

Use a bead of clear silicone caulk to secure the glass panes when you install them. This is so much easier than using glazing points or glass moldings. Additionally, it keeps the glass from rattling in the door frame. Apply caulk to both the rabbet and the back surfaces of the muntins.

If you have built a large bookcase and you want to hang it, attach a ledger to the wall, driving lag screws through the wallboard and into the studs. Rest the bottom (fixed) shelf on the ledger and have someone hold it in place while you attach the nailing strip to the wall.

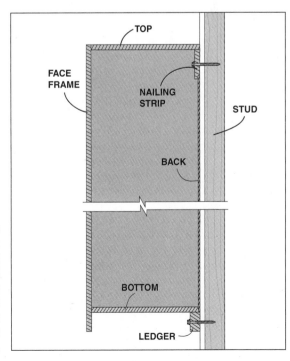

ALTERNATIVES ■ *Door Frame Joinery*

There are several joints you can use to assemble door frame members. Your choice depends on the size of the door, whether or not it incorporates molded surfaces, and whether it will have a wooden panel or a glass panel. Here are four possibilities.

CORNER LAP

Although not a traditional choice, lap joints are surprisingly strong, especially when rails and stiles are slender. These are best used for glazed doors.

1 Make a corner lap by cutting a rabbet in the ends of the adjoining boards. The rabbets must be half as deep as the thickness of the boards.

2 Glue the rabbeted ends of the boards together.

3 After the glue dries, rabbet the inside edge of the frame to hold a glass pane.

BRIDLE JOINT

Good for small and medium-sized doors, bridle joints can be made entirely on a table saw with just a saw blade. They are useful for both glazed and paneled doors.

1 To make a bridle joint, begin by cutting grooves in the inside edges of the frame members. Using a rip blade, cut a kerf in the edge, then turn the board around and cut another next to it. The kerfs will create a groove centered in the edge.

2 Cut the slot mortise in the same way. Using a tenoning jig to hold the board on end, cut a deep kerf in the end of the board, then turn the board around and cut another.

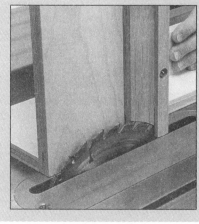

3 Cut the cheeks of the tenons with the boards held on end in a tenoning jig. Then lay the boards flat on the saw and cut the shoulders.

HAUNCHED MORTISE AND TENON

This is the traditional choice for paneled doors. It's a strong joint for doors of all sizes.

1 To make a haunched mortise and tenon, first cut a groove along the inside edges of the frame members.

2 Create the mortises in the stiles by drilling a line of overlapping holes, then shaving the sides and ends square with a chisel.

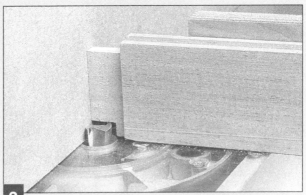

3 Cut the shoulders and cheeks of the tenon, then make a small notch or "haunch" in the top edge of the tenon.

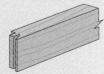

COPE-AND-STICK JOINT

This joint is commonly used for doors with molded or shaped surfaces. The adjoining frame members are cut to a mirror image of the molded profile.

1 A cope-and-stick joint requires a special set of matched router bits or shaper cutters. First, cut a groove and a molded profile in the inside edges of the frame members.

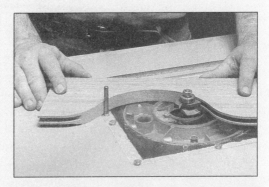

2 With the matching cutter, cut tenons with shaped or coped shoulders in the ends of the rails. The tenon will fit the grooves, and the coped shoulders will mate with the molded surfaces of the stiles.

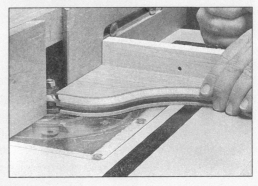

A BONUS PROJECT

Book Slip

Not long ago, a good friend of mine loaned Jim and me a rare book — a do-it-yourself guide for farmers from the turn of the century. The pages were in good condition, but as so often happens with well-used books, the binding had begun to separate. To return the favor of the loan, we made him this book slip to help protect his antique.

A book slip is just a box, made from a handsome hardwood. It's open at the front, and the sides have semi-circular reliefs to make it easier to grasp the book and pull it out of the slip.

MAKING THE PARTS The slip shown is made from figured cherry, but you can use any good hardwood. If you have some small pieces left over from a larger project that were just too precious to throw away, this would be a good time to dig them out. Depending on the size of the book, you can make a slip from just 2 or 3 board feet of lumber — less than that if you resaw the wood before planing it.

All the parts are made from ³/₈-inch-thick stock. The remaining dimensions are variable, depending on the size of the book. Figure the *inside* dimensions of the box by measuring the book. The thickness of the book is the inside width of the box; add ⅛ inch to its height and width for the box's height and depth.

Cut the parts to size, then rout ³/₁₆-inch-wide, ³/₁₆-inch-deep grooves near the back edges of the top, bottom, and sides. These grooves must be *stopped* — that is, they must not be cut from edge to edge. Instead, stop the router ³/₁₆ inch from each edge. If you cut all the way through to the edges, the ends of the grooves will be visible when you assemble the box.

Cut ³/₁₆-inch-wide, ³/₁₆-inch-deep rabbets all around the perimeter of the back. This will create tongues that fit the grooves, holding the back in place. **Note: To allow for expansion and contraction, the back should be slightly smaller across the grain than the actual dimensions would indicate. How much smaller? That depends on the thickness of the book. If the book is 3 inches thick or less, ¹/₁₆ inch should allow plenty of room for wood movement.**

Jim cut the through dovetails with the aid of a routing jig. Most of these jigs work on the same principle. As you rout, follow a template or "comb" with a guide collar. Cut the tails with a dovetail bit, and the pins with a straight bit. Cut both the tails and pins about ¹/₃₂ inch long so they slightly protrude when you assemble the parts. **Note: If you don't want to make dovetails, finger joints and splined miters serve equally well.**

After making the joinery, cut the reliefs in the sides with a band saw or scroll saw.

ASSEMBLING THE SLIP Finish sand the parts, then glue the top, bottom, and sides together. As you assemble these parts, slip the back into its grooves. However, *don't* glue the back in place. Let it "float" in the grooves, free to expand and contract.

Let the glue dry completely, then apply a finish. I recommend shellac — it's a benign chemical that doesn't react with other finishes. Nor does it seem to affect glues, inks, or papers. Consequently, there is little danger that it will harm the book that is stored in the slip.

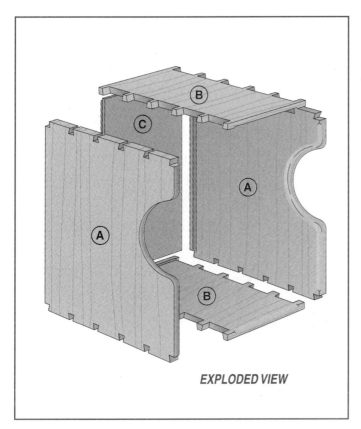

EXPLODED VIEW

BOOK SLIP ■ *MATERIALS LIST* (Finished Dimensions)

PARTS

A	Sides (2)	$\frac{3}{8}''$ × (variable) × (variable)
B	Top/bottom (2)	$\frac{3}{8}''$ × (variable) × (variable)
C	Back	$\frac{3}{8}''$ × (variable) × (variable)

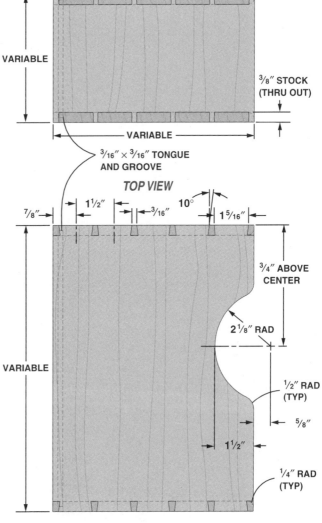

VARIABLE

$\frac{3}{8}''$ STOCK (THRU OUT)

VARIABLE

$\frac{3}{16}'' \times \frac{3}{16}''$ TONGUE AND GROOVE

TOP VIEW

$\frac{7}{8}''$ $1\frac{1}{2}''$ $\frac{3}{16}''$ 10° $1\frac{5}{16}''$

$\frac{3}{4}''$ ABOVE CENTER

VARIABLE

$2\frac{1}{8}''$ RAD

$\frac{1}{2}''$ RAD (TYP)

$\frac{5}{8}''$

$1\frac{1}{2}''$

$\frac{1}{4}''$ RAD (TYP)

SIDE VIEW

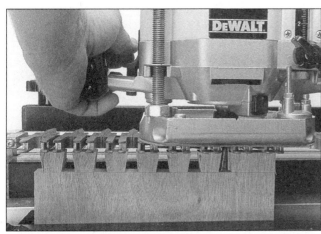

To rout through dovetails, you must make the joint in two steps. Secure the tail board vertically in the jig and fasten the tail comb over it. Rout the tails with a dovetail bit, guiding the router along the comb with a guide collar.

Making the pins in the pin board is similar, but you must switch to the pin comb. Cut the pins with a straight bit, following the comb.

Built-In Bookcase

In this chapter...

PRACTICAL KNOW-HOW

Standard Dimensions for Built-In Units	26
Cupboard Doors	34
Adjustable Shelving Supports	38
Trimming Out Built-Ins	41

JIGS AND FIXTURES

Corner Squares	33

SHOP SOLUTIONS

Double-Cutting Sheet Materials	30
Squaring a Case	33
Re-routing Heating Vents	40

Bookcases may be stand-alone, movable pieces of furniture; or they may be built in, permanently attached to the structure of your home. From the standpoint of a craftsman, the difference between the two may not be apparent. A built-in bookcase looks the same and relies on the same case construction techniques as a stand-alone unit. But if you look closer, you'll see that built-ins typically use lighter construction methods and materials, relying on the structure of your home to provide much of the support.

What size should it be?

Another difference between built-in and stand-alones is that built-ins are generally sized to fill the available space. Oftentimes, a built-in stretches from the floor to the ceiling or from wall to wall in a room.

When the space to be filled by a built-in is fairly large, craftsmen typically divide it up into smaller modules or units to simplify construction and installation. These units are arranged like building blocks in the space, then fastened to each other and to the building structure. You can use as many or as few units as you wish.

The built-in china cabinet above is sized so it reaches from the floor to the ceiling of the room in which it was installed. The bookcases and entertainment center below fill a corner in a den. This large installation is composed of three smaller units.

STANDARD DIMENSIONS FOR BUILT-IN UNITS

When designing a built-in bookcase system, there are basically two types of rectangular units you might use — a wall unit that hangs on a wall, or a standing unit that rests on the floor. Wall units tend to be smaller and less deep than standing units for the simple reason that it's more difficult to support a heavy unit when it's hanging on a wall.

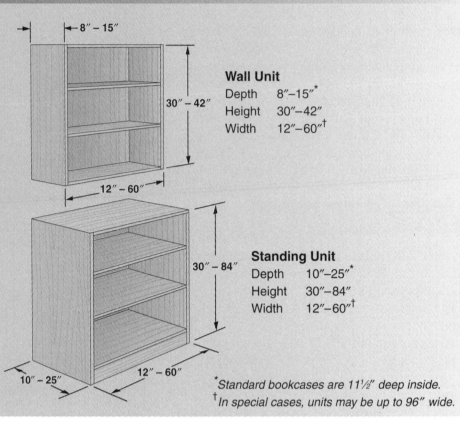

Wall Unit
Depth   8″–15″*
Height   30″–42″
Width   12″–60″†

Standing Unit
Depth   10″–25″*
Height   30″–84″
Width   12″–60″†

*Standard bookcases are 11½″ deep inside.
†In special cases, units may be up to 96″ wide.

DESIGN SAVVY ■ *Making a Built-In Turn a Corner*

Covering a wall with rectangular built-in units is a simple matter. But what if you want to turn a corner? There are several methods you can use. None of them are perfect; they all have their drawbacks. You must decide which one works best for you.

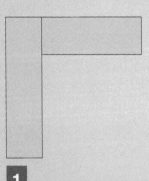

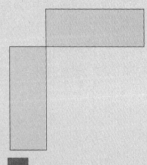

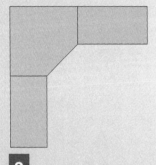

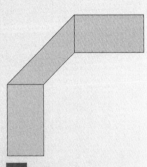

1 Butt the end of one unit against the face of another. *Drawback:* This makes the space in the corners hard to reach.

2 Install the units with the corners touching. *Drawback:* This wastes some space in the corner.

3 Build a five-sided corner unit. *Drawback:* The corner unit is much deeper than the adjoining units.

4 Build a unit with the ends set on diagonals. *Drawback:* This, too, wastes space in the corner.

What style will it be?

Because a built-in is attached to the structure of a house, most folks want the style to match the architecture. There are many different architectural styles, depending on the time period in which your home was built and the interior trim used. But most craftsmen lump these into just two categories.

TRADITIONAL STYLE

Built-in cases with face frames are called *traditional* cases. The doors that enclose the shelves are hinged to the face frames.

CONTEMPORARY STYLE

Built-in cases without face frames are said to be *contemporary*. The doors are hinged directly to the sides of the case.

SHAPE

In addition to the traditional and contemporary styles, built-in bookcases and shelving systems may take several different forms.

A *chimney* shape is straight up and down. The units are made in the shape of a simple rectangle. Or, if the system is divided into top and bottom units, they are all the same width and depth.

A *step-back* shape is customarily divided horizontally into two units. The top unit is not as deep as the bottom, forming a step between the two.

A *breakfront* is divided vertically into three units. The middle section is deeper (and often taller) than the flanking units.

CHIMNEY

STEP-BACK

BREAKFRONT

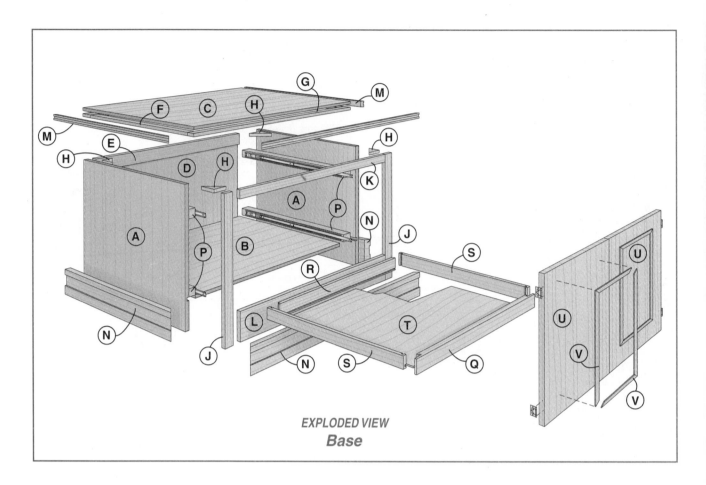

EXPLODED VIEW
Base

BUILT-IN BOOKCASE ■ *MATERIALS LIST* (Finished Dimensions)

PARTS — BASE

A	Sides (2)	$\frac{3}{4}'' \times 28\frac{1}{4}'' \times 34\frac{1}{2}''$
B	Bottom shelf	$\frac{3}{4}'' \times 28'' \times 40\frac{3}{4}''$
C	Top	$\frac{3}{4}'' \times 29\frac{1}{4}'' \times 42''$
D	Back	$\frac{1}{4}'' \times 27\frac{1}{2}'' \times 40\frac{3}{4}''$
E	Nailing strip	$\frac{3}{4}'' \times 3'' \times 40''$
F	Side top spacers (2)	$\frac{3}{4}'' \times 1\frac{1}{2}'' \times 26\frac{1}{4}''$
G	Front/back top spacers (2)	$\frac{3}{4}'' \times 1\frac{1}{2}'' \times 42''$
H	Corner braces (4)	$\frac{3}{4}'' \times 6'' \times 6''$
J	Face frame stiles (2)	$\frac{3}{4}'' \times 2'' \times 34\frac{1}{2}''$
K	Face frame top rail	$\frac{3}{4}'' \times 2'' \times 37\frac{1}{2}''$
L	Face frame bottom rail	$\frac{3}{4}'' 7\frac{3}{4}'' \times 37\frac{1}{2}''$
M	Top trim (total)	$\frac{3}{4}'' \times 1\frac{1}{2}'' \times 108''$
N	Base trim (total)	$\frac{3}{4}'' \times 7'' \times 108''$
P	Slide mounts (4)	$1\frac{1}{2}'' \times 2'' \times 28''$
Q	Shelf fronts (2)	$\frac{3}{4}'' \times 2\frac{1}{2}'' \times 37''$
R	Shelf backs (2)	$\frac{1}{2}'' \times 2\frac{1}{2}'' \times 35\frac{1}{2}''$
S	Shelf sides (4)	$\frac{1}{2}'' \times 2\frac{1}{2}'' \times 27''$

T	Shelf bottoms (2)	$\frac{1}{4}'' \times 26\frac{1}{2}'' \times 35\frac{1}{2}''$
U	Doors (2)	$\frac{3}{4}'' \times 18\frac{3}{4}'' \times 24\frac{3}{4}''$
V	Door molding (total)	$\frac{1}{4}'' \times \frac{3}{4}'' \times 66''$

HARDWARE

#8 × 1¼" Flathead wood screws (10)

#10 × 1¾" Flathead wood screws (4)

#10 × 2" Flathead wood screws (12)

#6 Pocket screws (4)

¾" Brads (20–24)

28" Full extension slides and mounting screws (2 pair)

No-mortise hinges and mounting screws (2 pair)

Door pulls (2)

Magnetic catches (2)

Note: This project can be easily sized to fit the available space in your home simply by altering the length and width of the parts.

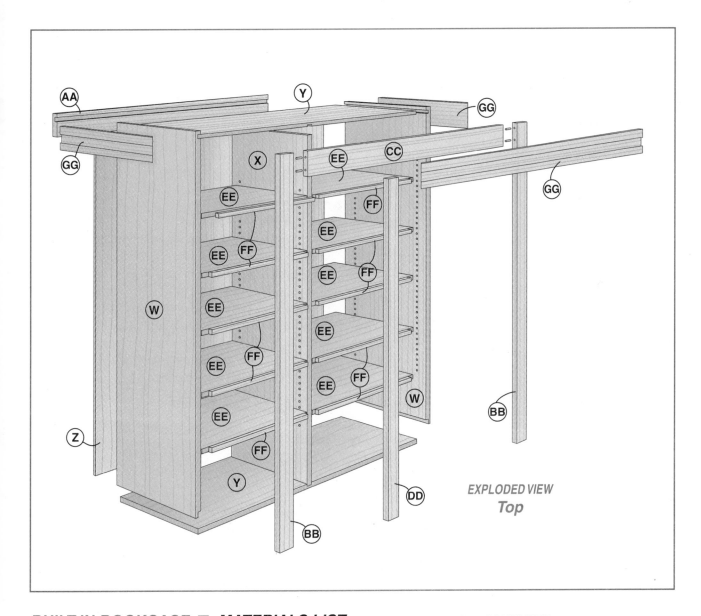

EXPLODED VIEW
Top

BUILT-IN BOOKCASE ■ *MATERIALS LIST* (Finished Dimensions) — *CONTINUED*

PARTS — TOP

W	Sides (2)	³/₄″ × 14¹/₂″ × (variable)
X	Divider	³/₄″ × 14¹/₄″ × (variable)
Y	Top/bottom shelf (2)	³/₄″ × 14¹/₄″ × 40³/₄″
Z	Back	¹/₄″ × 40³/₄″ × (variable)
AA	Nailing strip	³/₄″ × 3″ × 40″
BB	Outside face frame stiles (2)	³/₄″ × 2″ × (variable)
CC	Top face frame rail	³/₄″ × 4″ × 37¹/₂″
DD	Middle face frame stile	³/₄″ × 2″ × (variable)
EE	Adjustable shelves (10)	³/₄″ × 14¹/₄″ × 19¹/₂″
FF	Adjustable shelf trim (10)	³/₄″ × ³/₄″ × 17⁵/₈″
GG	Top molding (total)	³/₄″ × 4″ × 72″

HARDWARE

#8 × 1¹/₄″ Flathead wood screws (10)

#6 Pocket screws (4)

³/₈″ × 2″ Dowel pins (4)

¹/₄″ Shelving support pins (40)

Note: Those dimensions marked "variable" depend on the height of the ceiling in your home. Cut them so the top of the sides will be ¹/₄ to ¹/₂ inch short of the ceiling.

How do I build it?

Lloyd Bowser, a wonderfully talented finish carpenter and a good friend, made this built-in bookcase for my partner, Linda Watts. She and Lloyd worked out the design to fit the space in her front room and to match the interior architecture. The bookcase is made in two pieces — the bottom cupboard (or *base*) and the top shelves. The bottom portion is deeper than the top to create a step. They chose a traditional step-back style. The cases have a face frame, making the bookcase a traditional construction.

PREPARING THE MATERIALS

Because this bookcase was going to be painted, Lloyd didn't bother to make it from expensive hardwood and plywood with matching veneers. Instead, he used solid but inexpensive material that he knew would take the paint well. The plywood parts in this project are cabinet-grade birch, while the wooden parts are poplar.

Once you have the materials, double-check your measurements. Then plane the lumber to the necessary thicknesses — ½ and ¾ inch — and cut the parts to size.

TRY THIS!

When measuring a room for a built-in, make a vertical and horizontal *storystick* for each wall. On these sticks, mark the locations of windows, doors, outlets, moldings, and other important features in the room. Take these storysticks to the shop with you for reference. When you need to double-check a measurement, refer to the storysticks. This beats running back and forth between the room and the shop.

SHOP SAVVY ■ Double-Cutting Sheet Materials

To saw up large sheets of plywood and particleboard safely *and* accurately, try the double-cut method. Cut the sheet materials to rough size with a handheld circular saw, then cut it to final size on a table saw.

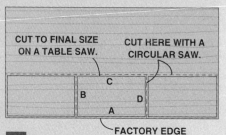

1 Lay out the parts on the sheet so each part has at least one *factory edge* (A). With a circular saw, cut the parts ¼ to ½ inch wider and longer than needed.

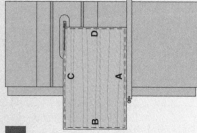

2 Using the rip fence as a guide, cut edge C directly opposite the factory edge. Don't cut the part to its final width yet; leave it just a little wide.

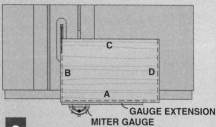

3 Trim edge B, using a miter gauge extension to help guide the work. Again, don't trim the stock to its final dimension; leave it a little long.

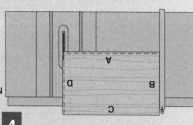

4 Trim edge D, using either the rip fence or the miter gauge to guide the cut. This time, cut the stock to its final length.

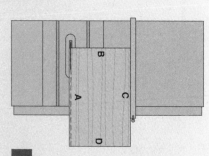

5 Trim the factory edge A, cutting the part to its final width.

BUILDING THE BASE UNIT

Lloyd, like most carpenters, likes to work from the ground up, so he started building this project with the base unit.

MAKING THE JOINERY Once the parts are cut to size, cut the joinery in the sides. There is actually very little joinery to make — just rabbets to hold the back and dadoes to hold the bottom shelf. You must also decide on a way to attach the nailing strip to the sides. Lloyd drilled screw pockets in the ends of the strip, but you might also use dowels, biscuits, or splines.

Also cut the joinery to join the members of the face frame. Here, Lloyd used dowels, but biscuits and pocket screws would work just as well. Traditionally, face frames were joined with lap joints or mortises and tenons.

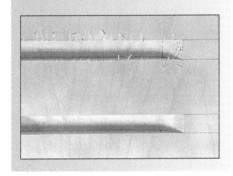

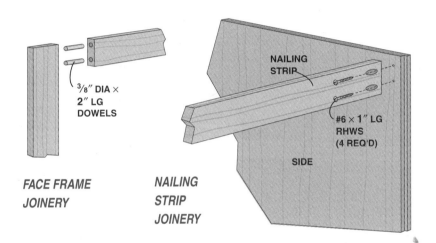

FACE FRAME JOINERY

NAILING STRIP JOINERY

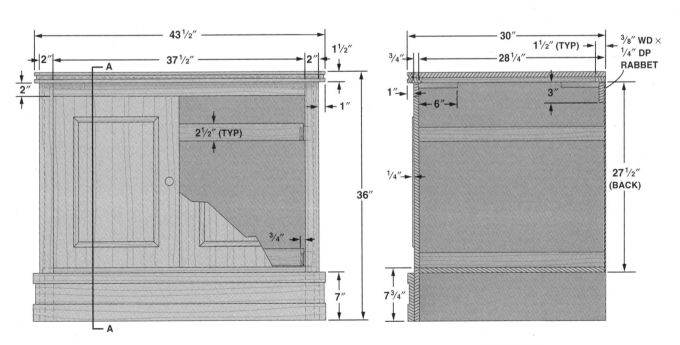

FRONT VIEW

SECTION A
(WITHOUT DRAWERS)

MAKING THE SLIDE MOUNTS The sliding shelves travel in and out of the base on extension slides. In a contemporary cabinet, you can mount these slides directly to the sides of the case, but in a traditional cabinet, you can't. The face frame will interfere with the action of the slides. Instead you must mount them on wooden blocks. Lloyd cut these particular blocks so they would protrude ¼ inch past the inside edge of the face frame. This keeps the slides from hanging up on the doors.

ASSEMBLING THE CASE After cutting all the parts and the joinery, assemble the case. Fasten the slide mounts to the sides with screws. Then glue the sides, bottom shelf, and nailing strip together. Install braces at each of the corners, flush with the top edge, attaching them with glue and screws.

Glue the face frame members together and attach the face frame to the front edges of the case. Glue the spacers around the perimeter of the top, on the underside. Attach the top to the case by driving screws up through the braces and into the top spacers.

Note: Wait until after you have installed the cases in your home to add the trim and molding.

TRY THIS!

If you are installing the bookcase in a home with uneven walls, you may need to build the units with a *fitting allowance* where they butt against the walls. This lets you trim the case to fit the wall. If you need fitting allowance at the back of a unit, cut the rabbet for the back slightly deeper than the back is thick. If you need it at the sides, build the face frame to overlap the sides.

How much fitting allowance is needed? Hold a straight board against the wall where the unit will be installed, using a level to make sure it's plumb. Measure the widest gap between the board and the wall — this is the allowance you need.

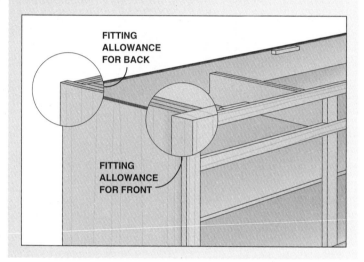

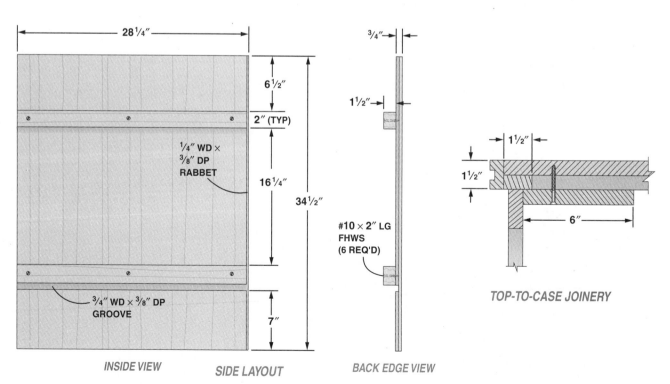

INSIDE VIEW   SIDE LAYOUT   BACK EDGE VIEW

NO PROBLEM ■ *Squaring a Case*

You carefully cut the parts and joinery as true as possible, but when you assemble the project, the case is out of square. No problem. As long as you identify the problem before the glue dries, it's an easy fix — just move the clamps.

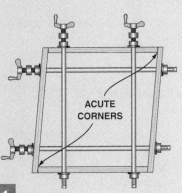

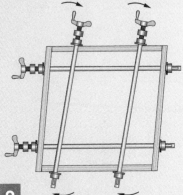

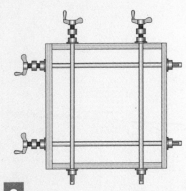

1 Check the assembly with a square and find the *acute* corners (where the angle is less than 90 degrees).

2 Loosen one or two of the clamps and angle them slightly toward the acute corners.

3 Slowly tighten the clamps, checking the corners as you do so. When the clamps pull the assembly square, stop tightening.

QUICK FIXTURE ■ *Corner Squares*

These simple fixtures are more useful than might first appear. I made a set of four corner squares to help keep boxes and cases square when I was gluing them up. But I quickly found they were invaluable fitting and assembly tools as well. With the aid of a few clamps, each corner square will hold two pieces at right angles to each other while you fit and mark joints. Or, you can use several to hold the parts of a project together during a dry assembly.

The corner squares are small pieces of plywood cut in the shape of a right triangle. Glue cleats to the sides of the triangle so you can clamp it to wooden boards. Cut a notch at the corners to keep the fixture clear of any glue that might squeeze out of a joint during assembly.

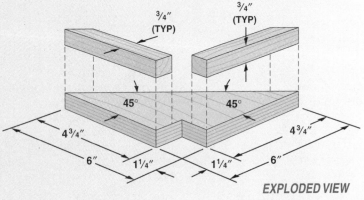

EXPLODED VIEW

ALTERNATIVES ■ *Cupboard Doors*

In a built-in system, those storage units or shelves that are enclosed by solid doors are typically called cupboards. There are many ways to make, fit, and hang doors on cupboards, depending on the look you want and how you prefer the doors to operate.

DOOR CONSTRUCTION

A slab door is made from a single sheet of plywood or particleboard. Often, the edges are banded to hide the plies.

A board-and-batten door is made from boards held together with cross ties or battens.

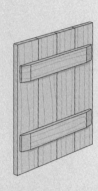

A frame-and-panel door is a wooden frame that holds a large wooden panel. The frame is dimensionally stable, but it allows the panel within it to expand and contract.

FITTING DOORS

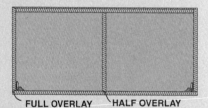

FULL OVERLAY   HALF OVERLAY

Inset doors are set into the case so the surface of the door is flush with the face frame or the front edges of the case.

Overlay doors cover the front surfaces of the case. Where a door completely covers an edge of the case, it's a full overlay. If it only covers the edge partway, it's a half-overlay.

Lipped doors are rabbeted to form a lip at the edges. This lip covers the front surfaces of the case, while the rabbeted portion fits inside the door opening. Normally, a lipped door is rabbeted all around the perimeter, but when two lipped doors butt against each other, the adjoining edges are left square.

HANGING DOORS

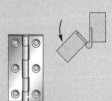

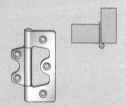

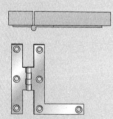

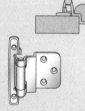

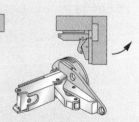

Butt hinges are installed between the door and the case. The leaves are recessed in shallow mortises.

No-mortise hinges also fit between the door and the case, but the thin leaves nest inside one another. This eliminates the need for mortises.

Overlay hinges have decorative leaves that lie on the surface of the door and case, straddling the seam between the two.

Offset hinges are designed for use with lipped doors. One leaf mounts to the front of the case, the other to the back side of the door.

European hinges remain completely hidden. One door leaf rests in a round mortise in the back side of the door, the other fastens to the inside case surface.

MAKING THE DOORS The doors in the base are slab doors, made from a single piece of plywood. Lloyd banded the plywood by gluing strips of veneer on the edges to hide the plies.

To give the doors some decoration, he applied strips of molding to the surfaces to form rectangles. This produced a visual effect similar to frame-and-panel doors.

FITTING AND HANGING THE DOORS Doors should be about ¹⁄₁₆ inch smaller than the door opening all around the perimeter. I usually make a door the same size as the opening, then plane the edges to fit .

But that technique won't work here. You cannot shave the edges of plywood doors after they are banded. Instead, cut them about ³⁄₃₂ inch smaller than the opening on all sides. When you add the veneer banding, which is about ¹⁄₃₂ inch thick, that will reduce the gap to the standard ¹⁄₁₆ inch.

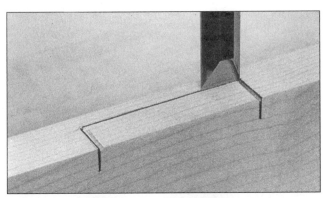

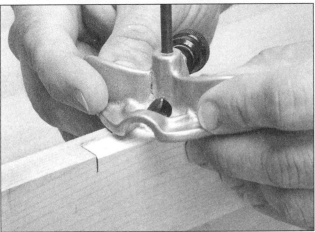

Here's an easy way to cut a hinge mortise. First, cut the edges of the mortise with a chisel and remove most of the waste *(top).* Then cut the bottom to a uniform depth with a *router plane (bottom).* This handy tool is available through most mail-order woodworking suppliers.

TRY THIS!

There are several glues formulated especially for applying moldings and decorative appliqués to wooden surfaces. Sometimes marketed as "craft" or "hobby" glues, these have a thicker consistency than ordinary aliphatic resin (yellow) and polyvinyl (white) glues. More important, they have a very short clamping time. You can apply a molding, hold it in place with your hands for a minute or two, then release the pressure and it will stay in place. These glues don't have the necessary strength for assembling cases, but they work well for decorative parts.

Wedge the doors in place in the case with toothpicks or wood slivers. Mark the location of the hinges on both the door and the face frame, scribing lines across the gap between the two. Using a chisel and a router plane, cut shallow mortises for the hinge leaves in the edge of the doors and the face frame.

If you'd rather not mess with mortises, try *no-mortise hinges.* The leaves are thinner than most butt hinges, and they nest inside one another when closed.

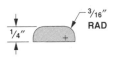

MOLDING PROFILE

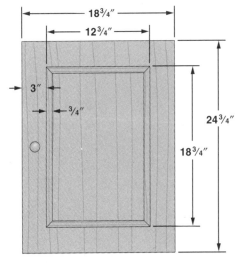

DOOR LAYOUT

MAKING THE SHELVES The "shelves" in the base unit are actually shallow drawers or trays. They are made like a box, with a front, back, sides, and bottom. The reason for this is that it helps keep things put when you slide the shelves in and out of the case. If the shelves were just a slab of wood, items might drop off the sides or the back.

Lloyd joined the front corners of the shelves with lock joints. Tenons on the ends of the shelf front fit dadoes in the sides. The joint is hidden or "blind" when you look at the assembled drawer from the front. The back corners are joined with rabbet-and-dado joints. These are similar to lock joints, but they aren't hidden. The drawer bottom "floats" in grooves cut into the inside surfaces of the front, back, and sides. Cut the joinery and assemble the shelves. After the glue dries, attach the full extension metal slides to them and mount them in the base unit.

Look Here! For more information on installing extension slides, see page 63.

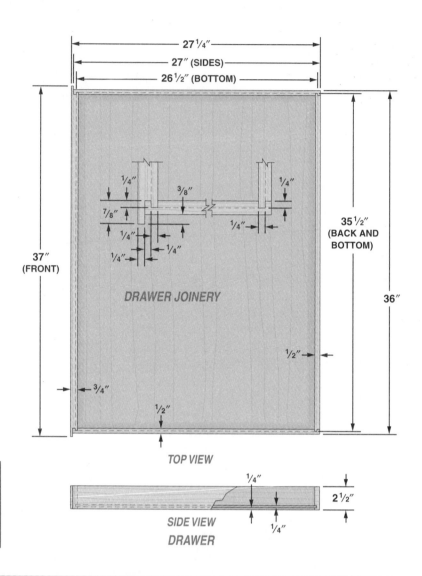

DRAWER JOINERY

TOP VIEW

SIDE VIEW
DRAWER

METHODS OF WORK ■ *Making a Lock Joint*

1 **To make a lock joint,** cut ¼-inch-wide, ⅞-inch-deep grooves in the ends of the drawer fronts, using either a table saw or a table-mounted router. A *tenoning jig* helps hold the work vertically.

2 **When you make** the grooves, you'll create two ⅞-inch-long tenons on each end of each drawer front. Cut the inside tongues short, making them just ¼ inch long.

3 **Cut** ¼-inch-wide, ¼-inch-deep dadoes near the ends of the drawer sides, on the inside surfaces. Fit the short tenons on the drawer front to these dadoes.

BUILDING THE TOP UNIT

The top unit is divided into two compartments. This reduces the span of the shelves, allowing you to make them from plywood or even particleboard. Had Lloyd omitted the divider, he would have made the shelves from hardwood to prevent them from sagging.

CUTTING THE JOINERY The top case is constructed in much the same way as the base. The top and bottom shelves rest in dadoes or rabbets in the sides. The divider rests in dadoes in the shelves. The back fits in rabbets at the back edges of the sides, and the nailing strip is attached with pocket screws. The only thing you haven't seen before is the notch in the upper back corner of the divider. This accommodates the nailing strip.

DRILLING SHELVING SUPPORT HOLES The adjustable shelves in the top rest on shelving support pins. These, in turn, fit in rows of holes in the sides and divider. Each row of holes has to be precisely the same as the other, with the holes on the same horizontal level. If one row is off, the shelves will tip and rock. To help drill these holes precisely, use a drilling guide.

> **Look Here! For more information on drilling guides, see page 15.**

TRY THIS!

To control the depth of the holes when using a drilling guide, fasten a stop collar to the drill bit.

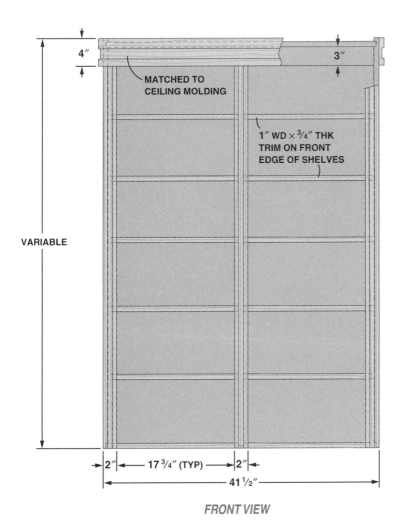

4"

MATCHED TO CEILING MOLDING

3"

1" WD × ³⁄₄" THK TRIM ON FRONT EDGE OF SHELVES

VARIABLE

2" ◄— 17³⁄₄" (TYP) —► 2"

◄———— 41¹⁄₂" ————►

FRONT VIEW

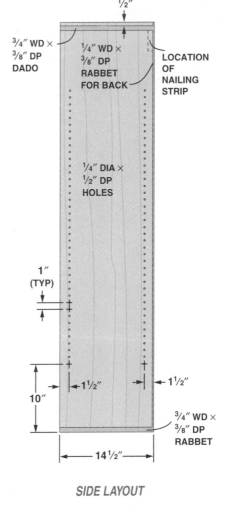

¹⁄₂"

³⁄₄" WD × ³⁄₈" DP DADO

¹⁄₄" WD × ³⁄₈" DP RABBET FOR BACK

LOCATION OF NAILING STRIP

¹⁄₄" DIA × ¹⁄₂" DP HOLES

1" (TYP)

10"

◄— 1¹⁄₂"   ◄— 1¹⁄₂"

³⁄₄" WD × ³⁄₈" DP RABBET

◄———— 14¹⁄₂" ————►

SIDE LAYOUT

MAKING THE FACE FRAME Join the face frame members for the top units with dowels, biscuits, or pocket screws. Note that this frame doesn't have a bottom rail. Consequently, it will be fairly fragile until you can attach it to the case. When the glue dries, set it aside where it won't be bumped.

TRY THIS!

While glue is usually sufficient to hold fixed shelves in dadoes, there are times when you need to reinforce the joint with wood screws. Drive the screws up through the shelf and into the adjoining part at an angle. This will hide the screws in the assembled shelving unit.

METHODS OF WORK ■ *Making a Dowel Joint*

1 To make a dowel joint, match up the mating surfaces of the adjoining boards and clamp them together. Draw pencil lines across the seam between the boards, wherever you want to install a dowel.

2 Align a doweling jig with a mark on one of the boards and clamp it in place. Use it like a drilling guide, boring a stopped hole at the mark. Repeat for each mark on each board.

3 Dry assemble the dowel joint (without glue) to check the alignment of the holes. If a hole is misaligned, fill it with a dowel and drill it again.

ALTERNATIVES ■ *Adjustable Shelving Supports*

There are several ways to install adjustable shelves in a bookcase. The method you choose depends on the design of the case and your own preferences.

The most common support hardware is **shelving support pins**. These fit in ¼-inch-diameter holes in the vertical parts of the case. There are several different shapes of pins for both wood and glass shelves.

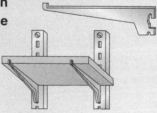

Standards may also hold **metal or wooden brackets**. With this method, the standards mount to the back of the bookcase.

Standards are metal strips with slots for clips. The standards can be installed in a groove or attached directly to the wood surface.

Wire supports also mount in holes in the vertical part of the case. The ends of the shelves are grooved to fit over the supports. The advantage of this method is that the hardware is hidden completely.

ASSEMBLING THE CASE Glue the sides, top and bottom shelves, and divider together. Check that the assembly is square as you clamp it together. Attach the nailing strip, driving pocket screws through the strip and into the sides. For extra strength, drive flathead wood screws through the strip and into the divider. Attach the back to the case with brads, then glue the face frame to the front edges.

INSTALLING THE UNITS

Once you have built the top and base units, attach them to the structure of your home.

FINDING THE STUDS The first step in any built-in installation is to explore the structure beneath the walls of your home. In most cases, this means finding the studs. There are several ways to do this, ranging from pure voodoo to pure science.

On the scientific side, you can invest in an electronic stud finder. I have one of these, and I'm reasonably happy with it, but I also have found that it doesn't work in every case. So I frequently resort to some effective voodoo called the "hunt and peck" method. You simply tap on the wall and listen for a "solid" sound that indicates the presence of a stud.

When you find a stud — by whatever method — mark it.

LEVELING THE UNITS Place the base where you want to install it and check that it's level. If it's not, insert small wedges beneath the bottom edges until the base rests level. Trace the slope and contour of the wall and floor on the case, then cut the

fitting allowance you have built into the case to match. Once cut, the base will sit level with the edges butted against the wall. Repeat for the top unit, cutting just those edges that you want to rest against the wall.

You don't always need to do this cutting, particularly if the built-in will be trimmed out with moldings. The molding will hide any ugly gaps between the walls, floors, ceiling, and the built-in. Instead, just level the case with wedges. I usually apply a little glue to the wedges so they stick to the edges of the case. Once the glue is dry, I trim them even with the case using a flush-cut saw.

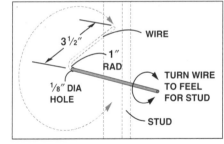

To find the studs in a wall, tap the wall with a small hammer. As you tap nearer the stud, the pitch rises sharply. When you think you know where a stud is, bore a small hole. Don't worry if you have to make several holes to find the stud — if the installed built-in doesn't cover them, fill them with Spackle. If the stud eludes you after boring several holes, try feeling for it with a bent wire.

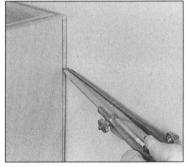

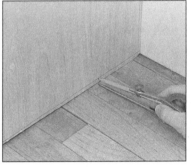

Trace the slope and contour of an uneven wall with a compass. After leveling the case, adjust the compass so the distance between the point and the scribe is equal to the widest gap between the case and the wall. Place the compass point against the wall and draw it along the surface, scribing the contour of the case. Repeat for the floor at the bottom of the case.

Trim the sides and bottom along the lines you have scribed. When you set the case in place again, it will rest level on the floor and butt solidly against the wall.

ATTACHING THE UNITS Remove the top from the base unit, if you haven't done so already. If, after positioning and leveling the base, the back doesn't rest flush against the wall, insert shims between the nailing strip and the wall wherever you've marked the stud locations. If your built-in has two or more base units and the face frames have a fitting allowance that protrudes beyond the sides slightly, the sides won't butt together. Place shims between the units to fill the gaps.

Fasten the adjoining sides of the units to one another with wood screws. Then attach them to the wall with nails, lag screws, or long wood screws,

driving the fasteners through the nailing strips and into the wall studs. Replace the tops.

Place the top unit on top of the base and fasten the two units together by driving finishing nails through the bottom shelf and into the base top. Set the heads of the nails. Then fasten the top nailing strip to the wall.

If the face frames of two adjoining base units have a fitting allowance, place shims between the sides. The thickness of the shims should equal the gap between the units. Fasten the sides together with wood screws, driving screws through the shims to hold them in place. After the sides are joined, trim the shims flush with the top edges of the sides.

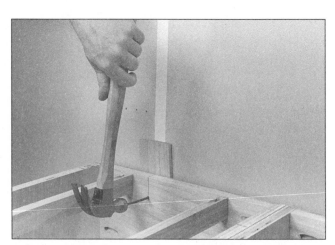

If the units stand out from the wall, place shims between the nailing strip and the wall. Fasten the cabinet to the wall, driving nails or screws through the nailing strips and shims and into the studs. Trim the shims flush with the top edges of the unit.

NO PROBLEM ▪ *Re-routing Heating Vents*

You're planning a built-in bookcase and discover that the base units will cover a heating vent. Moving the vent and modifying the ductwork would be a nightmare. No problem. You can easily re-rout the airflow from the vent to the front of the base unit. From tin flashing or plywood, make a shallow box with one open end. The height of the box must be equal to or a little less than the distance from the floor to the bottom shelf in the unit. Fasten the box to the floor over the vent, with the open end pointing away from the wall. Cut an air outlet in the bottom front rail of the bookcase to match up with the open end of the box when the unit is installed. Cover the opening with decorative grillwork.

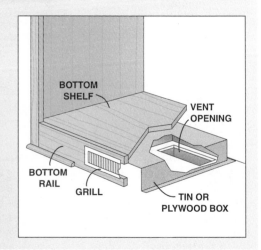

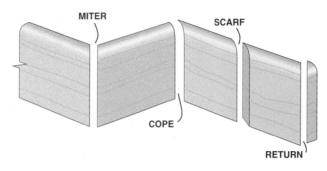

TRIMMING OUT BUILT-INS Once you've installed the units, trim your installation by adding the moldings and other decorative pieces. Note that the moldings Lloyd used to trim out his bookcase match those already in the room. This ties the built-in to the architecture, making it look like an integral part of the house.

Lloyd attached the trim to the bookcase with finishing nails, setting the heads of the nails below the surface of the wood. The joinery he uses to trim his built-ins is the same as any finish carpenter might employ to install molding in a room. Where the molding turns an outside corner, he uses a standard *miter joint*. On inside corners, he uses a *cope joint. Scarf joints* join lengths of molding to make long runs, and where a molding ends abruptly, he makes a *return*, which allows the profile to turn the corner and meet the wall.

FINISHING After the molding is installed, cover the heads of the finishing nails with putty or stick shellac. Then apply a finish to the built-in. In many cases, Lloyd finishes the units and trim *before* he installs them, then touches up the finish after installation.

METHODS OF WORK ■ *Installing Corner Molding*

To turn an *outside corner*, make a *miter joint*. Use a scrap of molding to mark the floor or ceiling where the outside surface will meet. Hold the molding in place and mark the outside of the miter where the lines cross. Mark the inside at the corner of the wall. Make a miter cut about 1/8 inch wide of the marks to see if the saw will pass through both. If it won't, shim the molding to adjust the angle of the cut.

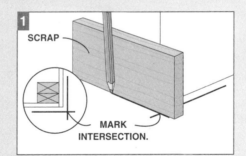

1 SCRAP

MARK INTERSECTION.

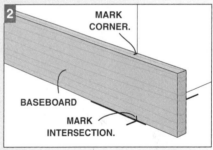

2 MARK CORNER.

BASEBOARD

MARK INTERSECTION.

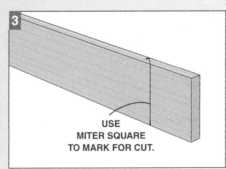

3 USE MITER SQUARE TO MARK FOR CUT.

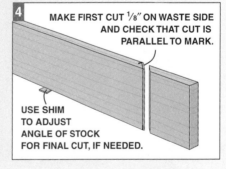

4 MAKE FIRST CUT 1/8" ON WASTE SIDE AND CHECK THAT CUT IS PARALLEL TO MARK.

USE SHIM TO ADJUST ANGLE OF STOCK FOR FINAL CUT, IF NEEDED.

To turn an *inside corner* when installing molding, use a *cope joint,* cutting one of the adjoining ends to a reverse shape of the molding so it fits tightly when butted against the other piece. To do this, miter the end of the part you wish to cope. With a coping saw or a scroll saw, cut along the arris where the mitered surfaces meet the profile.

Inset Shelves

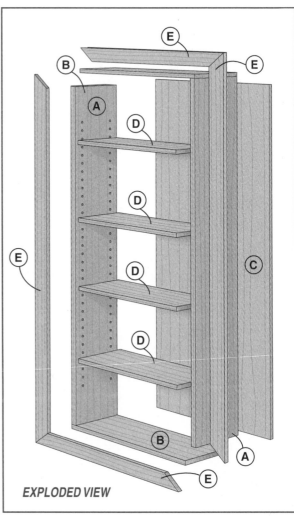

EXPLODED VIEW

INSET SHELVES ■ MATERIALS LIST
(Finished Dimensions)

PARTS

A	Sides (2)	¾″ × (variable) × (variable)
B	Top/Bottom (2)	¾″ × (variable) × (variable)
C	Back	¼″ × (variable) × (variable)
D	Shelves (3-6)	½″ × (variable) × (variable)
E	Molding	(all dimensions variable)

HARDWARE

Shelving support pins (4 per shelf)

#4 Finishing nails (12–20)

Here's another built-in shelving unit made by finish carpenter Lloyd Bowser. In this case the shelves are set into the wall, installed between the studs. By necessity, this is a small project. The width of the unit is limited by the space between the studs, normally 14½ to 22½ inches. The depth of the shelves can be no greater than the width of the studs in your walls (normally 3½ inches). This unit is slightly deeper because Lloyd not only built the shelves but also made the wall. Knowing that he was going to install inset shelves, he used 2 × 6 studs.

MAKING THE SHELVING UNIT

Locate the studs in the wall where you want to install the shelves. Cut out a small square plug, large enough to inspect the space between the studs with an inspection mirror. (Keep the plug in case you need to repair the hole.) Look for any wires or pipes that might interfere with your installation. If the space is unobstructed, enlarge the opening to the size you want to fill with shelves. Also verify the depth of the space.

Build a shallow box to fit between the studs with about 1/8 inch to spare on each side. (The molding will cover any gaps between the wall and the box.) Before you assemble the parts, drill rows of 1/4-inch-diameter holes in the box sides to accommodate shelving support pins. Trim the edges of the box

with a molding that matches or complements the architectural moldings in your home.

INSTALLING THE UNIT

Apply a mastic adhesive (such as *Liquid Nails*) to the back side of the molding and press the box into place. Because this is a small shelving unit, it probably won't need anything more to hold it securely. If the unit is large or you plan to use it to display your collection of paving bricks, secure it by driving wood screws through the sides and into the studs. Counterbore the heads of the screws, then cover them with wooden plugs.

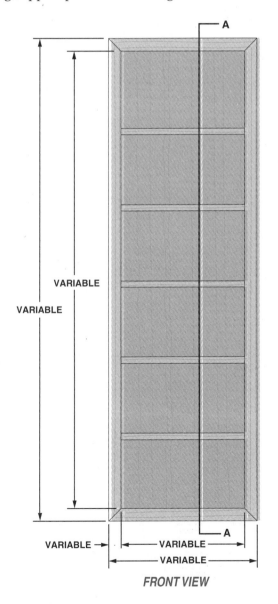

FRONT VIEW

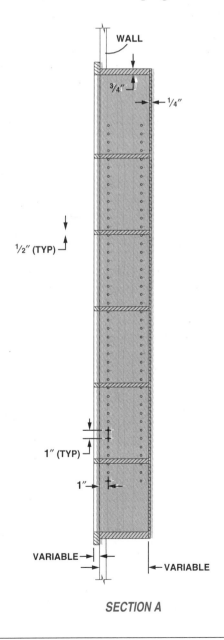

SECTION A

Quick-and-Easy Shelves

While bookcases are relatively straightforward projects, it has always amazed me that they take so much time to build and require so many materials. What do you do if you need a lot of shelving space, you want it to look good, but you don't want to spend a fortune on lumber and months of shop time putting it together?

Here's one possible answer. This attractive set of shelves, built by Marvin Olinsky and Joe McIntyre, is designed to be easy and inexpensive to build, yet it provides an enormous amount of shelving space. Despite its simplicity, it's a good-looking piece, done in the new Millennium furniture style.

Marvin's and Joe's shelves save lumber by using four L-shaped uprights at the corners to support the shelves. This eliminates the need for solid sides and a back. (As shown, the shelves require 65 board feet of lumber. Typically a bookcase this size would need 90 board feet.) The vertical strips at the sides prevent the books from falling off to the right or left, and the horizontal rails at the back keep the structure from racking side to side. In short, it's as rigid and as useful as any shelving unit, even though it requires a good deal less lumber to make it.

Look Here! For more information on the Millennium style, see page 9.

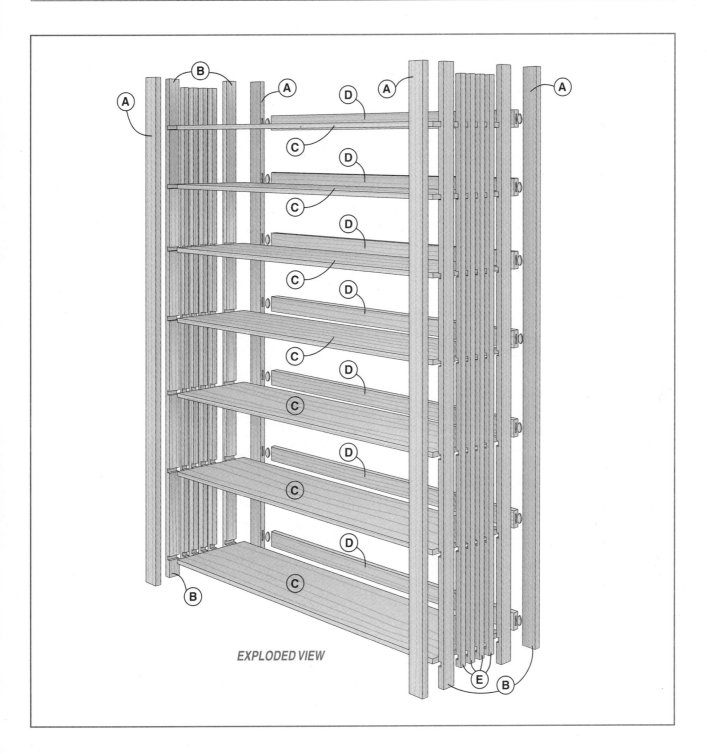

EXPLODED VIEW

QUICK-AND-EASY SHELVES ■ *MATERIALS LIST* (Finished Dimensions)

PARTS

A	Front/back legs (4)	$3/4'' \times 2'' \times 92''$
B	Side legs (4)	$3/4'' \times 1\,3/4'' \times 92''$
C	Shelves (7)	$3/4'' \times 11\,1/4'' \times 47\,1/4''$
D	Rails (7)	$3/4'' \times 3'' \times 44''$
E	Vertical strips (8)	$3/4'' \times 3/4'' \times 88\,1/4''$

HARDWARE

#20 Biscuits (14)

Note: As shown, the shelving unit is 48 inches wide and 92 inches tall. However, you can make it to any size simply by adjusting the length of the legs or the span of the shelves.

MAKING THE PARTS

To keep construction as simple as possible, all the parts are made from the same ¾-inch-thick stock, cut to simple rectangles. Cut the shelves, rails, front and back legs to size. Before you make the side legs and the vertical strips, cut the joinery in the stock. Select two boards at least 8 inches wide and cut them to the length of the side legs. Cut ¾-inch-wide, ⅜-inch-deep dadoes across the width of each board, spacing them as the shelves are spaced (shown in the *Front View*). After cutting the dadoes, rip the side legs and strips from the boards. Cut the strips 1½ inches shorter than the legs at the top and 2¼ inches shorter at the bottom.

Using one of the side legs as a "storystick," carefully mark the inside edges of the back legs where the rails will join them. Cut biscuit joints or dowel joints in the ends of the rails and edges of the back legs.

TRY THIS!

Cut the side legs and strips from each board in order, numbering them as you go. When you assemble the project, assemble these parts in order. The wood grain in the side parts will appear continuous.

ASSEMBLING THE SHELVES

Finish sand the parts. To save some work, Marvin and Joe recommend that you apply finish to the strips before you put the shelves together. Otherwise, it's a real bear to apply, sand, and rub out the finish between the strips. Carefully mask the dadoes with tape so you won't get finish on the surfaces that you want to glue later.

Assemble the legs first, gluing the front and back legs to the side legs to make L-shaped beams. Also glue the rails to the shelves.

Marvin tells me the next part of the assembly process is a two-person job. Get someone to help you, then lay two of the leg assemblies on the floor and attach the shelves to them. Glue the ends of the shelves in the dadoes and the ends of the rails to the edges of the legs. Glue the remaining two legs to the other ends of the shelves. Clamp the assembly together, bracing it so it remains square while the glue dries.

When the glue sets, remove the clamps and glue the vertical strips to the ends of the shelves, spacing them as shown in the *Side View*.

Let the glue dry completely, then apply a finish to those surfaces you haven't already finished.

The shelves rest in dadoes in the side legs and vertical strips. To ensure that these dadoes all line up, select two boards at least 8 inches wide to make the parts for the right and left sides. Cut the boards 92 inches long, then cut dadoes across the width, from edge to edge. The self-clamping Router Guide on page 14 helps make short work of this task.

After cutting the dadoes, rip the boards into narrow legs and strips.

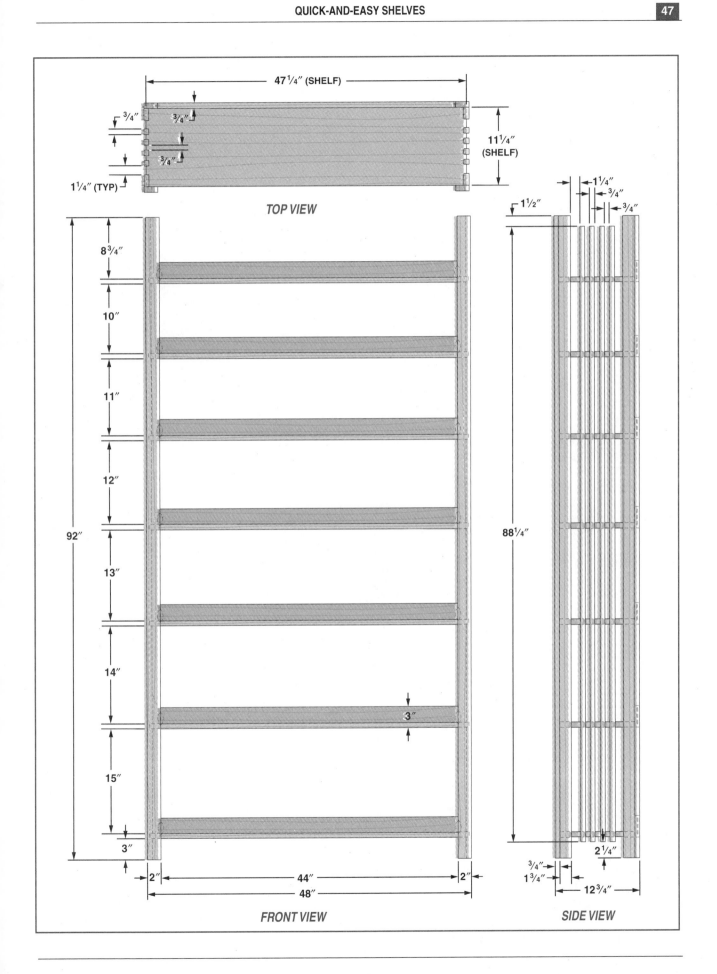

47¼″ (SHELF)

¾″

¾″

¾″

11¼″
(SHELF)

1¼″ (TYP)

TOP VIEW

8¾″

10″

11″

12″

92″

88¼″

13″

14″

3″

15″

3″

2″ 44″ 2″

48″

FRONT VIEW

1½″

1¼″

¾″

¾″

2¼″

¾″

1¾″

12¾″

SIDE VIEW

Rolltop Desk
(plus Filing Cabinets and a Pedestal Desk)

In this chapter...

PRACTICAL KNOW-HOW

Rolltop Styles	51
Desk Construction	52
Building the Pedestals	57
Making a Pedestal Desk	67
Making the Rolltop	73
Designing and Assembling Tamboured Doors	78

JIGS AND FIXTURES

Extension Slide Drill Guide	71

SHOP SOLUTIONS

Frame-and-Panel Construction	57
Routing Half-Blind Dovetails	62
Drawer Guides	63
Cabinets for Computers	64
Drawer Brackets	70
Laying Out an Oval	73
Making Lock Joints	82

Long ago, I learned the value of building large projects in small steps. If you plan these steps carefully, you can end up with something useful and pleasing at the end of each step. You don't get to your goal any quicker, but it's more enjoyable getting there.

This rolltop desk is designed to be built in three stages. During the first stage, you make the pedestals. These are short *filing cabinets,* and you can use them as such while you're working on the next stage. In fact, you can stop there if what you really need are filing cabinets. The second stage is to build a desktop and a middle drawer and join them to the cabinets to make a *pedestal desk.* Once again, you can stop at the desk if that's your aim. The last stage is to create pigeonholes and tambours for the desk, converting it into a *rolltop.*

What size should it be?

That depends on which component you're making and where you plan to stop.

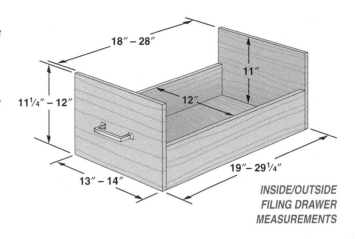

INSIDE/OUTSIDE FILING DRAWER MEASUREMENTS

SIZING FILING CABINETS To size a filing cabinet, begin with the drawers. The drawers must be wide enough and deep enough to hold standard file folders. Most are 12 inches wide and 11 inches tall (on the inside), allowing you to organize the folders from the front to the back of the drawer, in a single row. The depth of the drawer (from front to back) is usually between 18 and 28 inches. To make a two-drawer filing cabinet, you'll need a case 15 to 16 inches wide, 28 to 30 inches tall, and 20 to 30 inches deep.

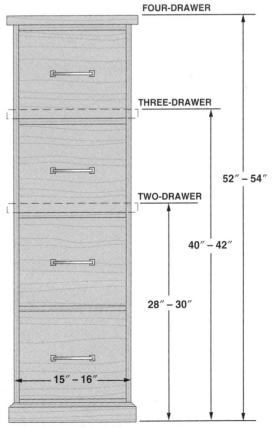

Ordinarily, files are organized front-to-back in a drawer *(top).* But if you need to make a narrow cabinet, you can organize them side-to-side *(left).*

FILING CABINET HEIGHTS

You can make the cabinet narrower by organizing the files side to side in two rows. That's what Jim and I did for this project. We wanted it to fit in a small space, so we couldn't make it very wide — just 52 inches. To maintain a comfortably sized kneehole (the space between the cabinets), the cabinet/pedestals couldn't be much wider than 14 inches.

SIZING A PEDESTAL DESK

The height of a desktop above the floor should be about 30 inches for general work, or 24 to 28 inches if it's used exclusively for typing or computer work. Often, pedestal desks have a smaller desk attached to one side, making an L-shaped work surface. The larger desktop is 30 inches above the floor, while the smaller is 27 inches for typing.

The surface itself should be broad enough to spread out your books and papers. Remember, desks accumulate an amazing amount of desktop accessories — lamps, reference books, bookends, staplers, tape dispensers, pencil holders, calculators, bowling trophies, and so on. Best make it bigger than you need to begin with; you'll find stuff to fill up the space. Generally, desktops are 24 to 32 inches wide and 48 to 60 inches long.

The size of the kneehole (the space between the pedestals) is extremely important to your comfort. To make room for your legs under the desk, it should be at least 20 inches wide, 12 inches deep, and 24 inches tall.

SIZING PIGEONHOLES

The structure on top of a rolltop — the *pigeonholes* — evolved from an old piece of furniture known as a *desk box*. It typically is divided up into small drawers and compartments to help you organize bills, letters, stationery, stamps, and all the other materials associated with a desk. A pigeonhole assembly should be placed toward the back of the desk, leaving at least 20 inches of free space in front. Although it can be any size that you want it to be, these assemblies are

usually no more than 12 to 14 inches tall and 8 to 10 inches deep. They often stretch the entire width of the desk. The size of individual compartments depends on their use. If a compartment is intended to organize bills and envelopes, it should be 2 to 3 inches wide and at least 4½ inches tall. Stationery compartments must be 12 inches wide and are only 1½ to 2 inches tall. A compartment housing a small drawer may be only 3 inches wide and 1½ inches tall.

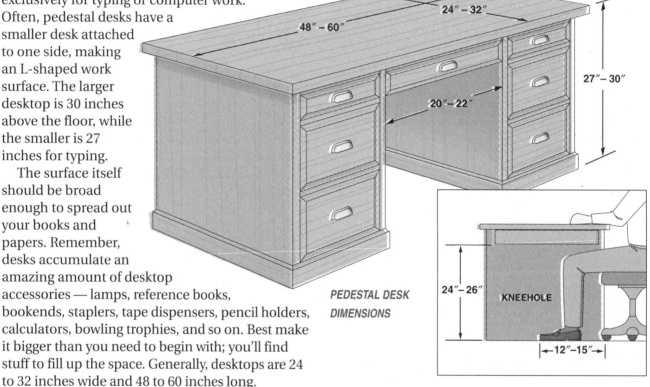

PEDESTAL DESK DIMENSIONS

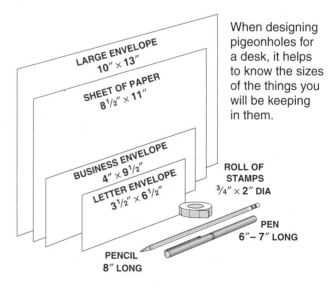

When designing pigeonholes for a desk, it helps to know the sizes of the things you will be keeping in them.

What style will it be?

Rolltop desks first appeared in the nineteenth century and have been produced in every style imaginable since then, from Federal to Postmodern. However, the style that almost everyone thinks of when they envision a rolltop is *Victorian Oak* — massive pedestals with either straight legs or a frame base, panel construction, all made from white oak and stained a rich, dark golden color. The rolltop in this chapter is typical of Victorian Oak design.

Once you've decided on a style, you must also determine a *shape* for the pigeonhole assembly atop the desk. On the earliest rolltops, this was a simple box. The tambours were mounted vertically to form a "curtain." When they opened, the curtain split in the center and slid to each side. However, during the Victorian Oak period, cabinetmakers began to mount the tambours horizontally. Over the next century, they developed three distinct shapes for the pigeonhole assembly.

ELLIPTICAL ROLLTOP DESK

The tambours can also follow a simple curve, usually an ellipse, at the front of the pigeonholes.

WATERFALL ROLLTOP DESK

When the rolltop is said to have a waterfall shape, the tambours follow a complex curve at the front of the pigeonholes. This curve reverses itself three times, curving down near the top, then leveling out, and finally turning down again to meet the desktop.

SLANT-FRONT ROLLTOP DESK

The tambours turn a short curve, then follow a straight line that slopes down to the desktop. This shape echoes the design of an older desk form, the slant-front secretary.

Crafted by Alan Wilkinson Fine Furniture, Pearl City, HI; photo by Jerry Chong

DESIGN SAVVY ■ *Desk Construction*

A desk is a highly personal work center, often engineered to accommodate the way just one particular person likes to work. For this reason, there are thousands of unique and imaginative desk designs to consider when you start to design your own desk. But for all this variety, there are really only four basic types:

- ■ Writing desk
- ■ Secretary
- ■ Pedestal desk
- ■ Workstation

With a few exceptions, almost every desk design you run across is a variation on one of these forms.

To design your own desk, select one basic form that appeals to you. Look through project and design books for *features* (rather than forms), selecting those that will be useful in the type of work you expect to do at a desk. Then incorporate those features into the form.

WRITING DESK

The earliest desks weren't what we like to think of as desks at all, but small boxes that held writing materials, correspondence, ledgers, and so on. Often, the tops were covered in leather and slightly sloped to provide a comfortable writing surface. When the owner of one of these writing boxes (or *lap desks,* as they came to be called) needed to use it, he placed it on a table. As the amount of paperwork increased, so did the size of the box. Eventually, folks began to attach their desk boxes to a table permanently. This form — a table with a storage box perched on top of it — became the *writing desk.*

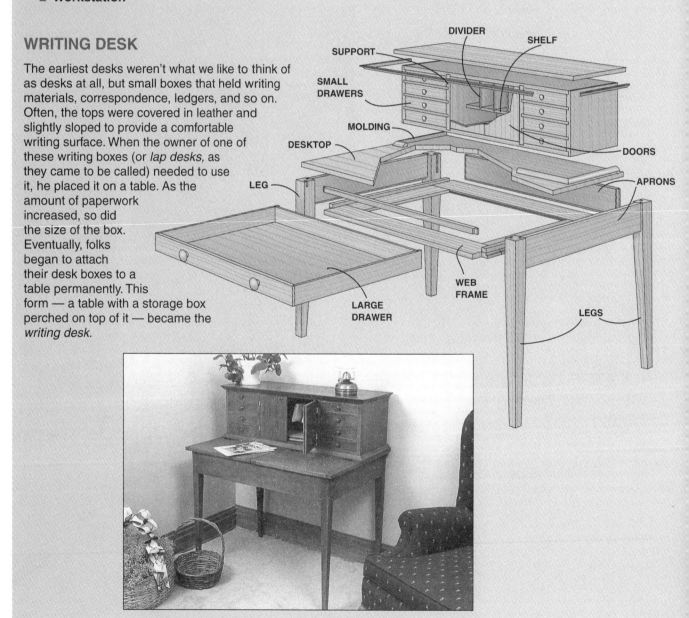

Crafted by George Reid

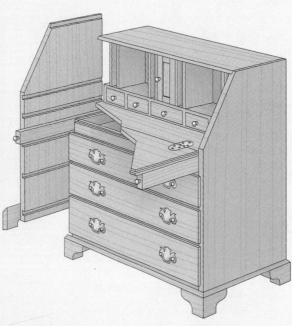

SECRETARY

About the same time that writing desks appeared, cabinetmakers began to adapt another furniture form to serve as a desk. They married a desk box to the top of a chest of drawers. The front of the box opened, dropping down to serve as a writing surface. This became known as a *secretary*.

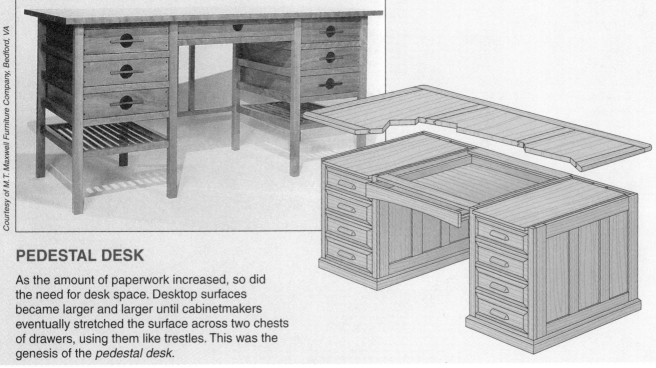

Courtesy of M.T. Maxwell Furniture Company, Bedford, VA

PEDESTAL DESK

As the amount of paperwork increased, so did the need for desk space. Desktop surfaces became larger and larger until cabinetmakers eventually stretched the surface across two chests of drawers, using them like trestles. This was the genesis of the *pedestal desk*.

(continued)

DESIGN SAVVY ■ *Desk Construction* — CONTINUED

COMPUTER WORKSTATION

The latest wrinkle in desk construction is the computer workstation. The purpose of a workstation is to hold computer components in the proper relationship to each other and to the computer operator. Most of the forms I've covered so far — writing desk, secretary, and pedestal desk — are simple and straightforward furniture pieces. But a workstation is a slightly different animal. You need to understand the ergonomics — the interface between the user and the machine — to build a good one. In that sense, it's more like a cockpit than a desk.

To design a workstation, consider each of the computer components it will hold.

CPU The placement of the central processing unit, or CPU — the heart of the computer — is, surprisingly, the least of your concerns. You must be able to reach the switches and the drives, but you can put the CPU anywhere within an arm's length.

Most operators place the CPU on the desktop, but this takes up valuable work space. It's often better to place it under the desktop or on the floor beside the workstation. When Jim and I made the rolltop desk for this chapter, we designed one of the pedestals to hold a computer "tower."

KEYBOARD The closer you put the keyboard to your lap, the more comfortable it will be to type. If the keyboard is too high, you must hold your arms up when you type, and they will tire quickly. Mount the keyboard 24 to 28 inches above the floor, the same height as a typing table. (Ideally, your elbows should make a 90-degree bend when typing.) If you spend long stretches at the computer, invest in a keyboard shelf that can be adjusted up or down. By adjusting the keyboard level from time to time, you forestall fatigue.

MOUSE Include a flat area next to your monitor for a mouse or trackball. A mouse requires an area about 10 inches square for maneuvering; a trackball needs a space about 5 inches by 5 inches. If both right- and left-handed people will be using the workstation, provide space on both sides of the keyboard.

MONITOR There are two schools of thought on where to put the monitor. At eye level, the strain on your neck is at a minimum, but the monitor and the keyboard are separated in your line of vision by as much as 60 degrees. You tire as you glance back and forth between your hands and the screen. If you place the monitor as close to the keyboard as possible, there's more neck strain

The purpose of a workstation is to hold all the computer components in an efficient and comfortable arrangement. If poorly arranged, even the best of systems will be tedious and tiring to use.

but less eyestrain. Some workstations incorporate a monitor shelf below the level of the keyboard so you see the monitor just over the edge of the keyboard.

Wherever you place the monitor, the screen should be at least 28 inches from your eyes (unless you have one of the newer "flat screen" monitors). The cathode ray tubes in standard monitors generate electro-

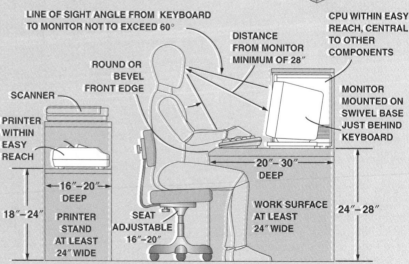

LINE OF SIGHT ANGLE FROM KEYBOARD TO MONITOR NOT TO EXCEED 60°

DISTANCE FROM MONITOR MINIMUM OF 28"

CPU WITHIN EASY REACH, CENTRAL TO OTHER COMPONENTS

ROUND OR BEVEL FRONT EDGE

SCANNER

PRINTER WITHIN EASY REACH

MONITOR MOUNTED ON SWIVEL BASE JUST BEHIND KEYBOARD

16"–20" DEEP

18"–24"

PRINTER STAND AT LEAST 24" WIDE

SEAT ADJUSTABLE 16"–20"

20"–30" DEEP

WORK SURFACE AT LEAST 24" WIDE

24"–28"

magnetic radiation. This may affect your health unless you maintain a respectful distance.

PRINTER If you like to read the printout as it rolls out of the printer, then you may want to place your printer below the work surface, 18 to 24 inches above the floor. This is becoming less and less of a concern, however. Some of the newer printers — especially inkjet and laser printers — won't allow you to read a page until after it's printed. If this is the case, you simply need to put the printer where you can easily reach the controls and the paper trays.

Many workstations are designed so the printer rests on a separate stand. This lets you put the printer where it works best for you. If you have limited space, you can also store it on a slide-out shelf beneath the desktop.

SCANNER The rules for the placement of a scanner are similar to that of a printer. It should be within easy reach, the controls must be accessible, and the level of the bed should be below your eye level (when seated) so you can see to arrange the materials you're scanning. The most comfortable height, I've found, is 24 to 34 inches above the floor.

FLEXIBILITY The most important feature you should include is flexibility. Make it easy to rearrange the position of the computer components by making the workstation modular and the shelves adjustable. This will help you keep up with rapidly changing technology.

This pedestal is designed to house a computer tower. What appears to be drawer fronts is actually a door with beveled appliqués. The door swings up and disappears into the pedestal case, much like the door on a barrister's bookcase.

This small shelving unit holds a printer and a scanner, one on top of the other. There are also a few shelves for paper and envelopes. The unit takes up only a slightly larger footprint on your desktop than one machine alone, allowing you to store two machines in the space of one.

When Jim and I completed the pedestal desk portion of this rolltop project, we divided the desktop into four separate surfaces. Two of the surfaces were mounted atop the pedestal so their height above the floor was 30 inches. The other two were suspended between the pedestals to serve as keyboard and monitor shelves. Since these shelves can be attached to the pedestal anywhere, you can adjust their height to suit yourself.

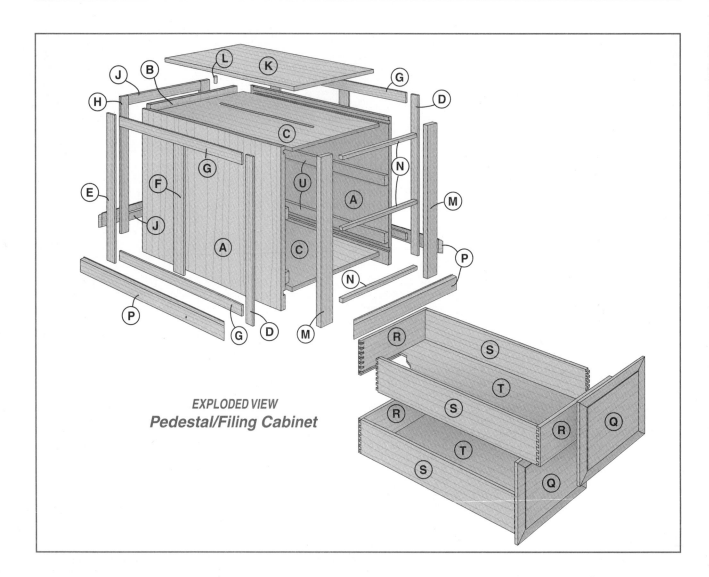

EXPLODED VIEW
Pedestal/Filing Cabinet

ROLLTOP DESK ■ *MATERIALS LIST* (Finished Dimensions)

PARTS — PEDESTAL/FILING CABINET (FOR ONE PEDESTAL ONLY)

A	Sides* (2)	$3/4'' \times 29'' \times 28\,5/8''$
B	Back*	$3/4'' \times$ (variable) $\times 28\,5/8''$
C	Top/bottom* (2)	$3/4'' \times$ (variable) $\times 28\,5/8''$
D	Side front stiles (2)	$1/4'' \times 1\,1/4'' \times 28\,5/8''$
E	Side back stiles (2)	$1/4'' \times 1\,3/4'' \times 28\,5/8''$
F	Side middle stiles (2)	$1/4'' \times 2'' \times 23\,3/4''$
G	Side rails (4)	$1/4'' \times 1\,1/2'' \times 26''$
H	Back stiles (2)	$1/4'' \times 1\,5/8'' \times 28\,5/8''$
J	Back rails (2)	$1/4'' \times 1\,1/2'' \times$ (variable)
K	Pull-out shelf	$3/4'' \times$ (variable) $\times 29\,3/4''$
L	Stop dowel	$1/2''$ dia. $\times 1''$
M	Face frame stiles (2)	$3/4'' \times 1\,5/8'' \times 28\,5/8''$
N	Face frame rails (3)	$3/4'' \times 3/4'' \times$ (variable)

P	Base molding (total)	$3/4'' \times 3'' \times 96''{-}104''$
Q	Drawer faces (2)	$3/4'' \times 11\,1/2'' \times$ (variable)
R	Drawer fronts/backs (4)	$1/2'' \times 6'' \times$ (variable)
S	Drawer sides (4)	$1/2'' \times 6'' \times 27\,3/4''$
T	Drawer bottoms* (2)	$1/4'' \times$ (variable) $\times 27\,1/2''$
U	Drawer mounts (4)	$5/8'' \times 2'' \times 29''$

*Make these parts from plywood.

HARDWARE

#6 × 1¼" Pocket screws (6)

Drawer pulls and mounting screws (2)

28" Full extension slides and mounting screws (2 sets)

How do I build it?

Decide what you want to build — a filing cabinet, pedestal desk, or a complete rolltop desk. If you opt for a filing cabinet, you probably want to use the dimensions shown on the *Wide Pedestal/Front View.* This will let you arrange files front to back. If you're building a desk, and the top is less than 60 inches wide, you must make narrower pedestals to keep the kneehole a comfortable width. Jim and I used the dimensions shown in the *Narrow Pedestal/Front View.*

BUILDING THE PEDESTALS

Jim made the pedestals from plywood and trimmed them with wooden strips to give them the appearance of traditional frame-and-panel construction. There are no frames or panels, however. The cases are just plywood boxes. The rails and stiles are thin pieces of wood glued directly to the plywood.

PREPARING THE MATERIALS Traditionally, rolltop desks are made from white oak. Ours is made from oak-veneer plywood and red oak. We considered making it from white oak, but white oak plywood is a special order at most lumberyards, and it costs an arm and a leg. So we decided on red oak because it was less expensive and easier to find. Besides, once

Split the 4/4 stock for the trim in half by *resawing* it on a band saw. Then plane the resawed boards to ¼ inch thick.

the oak is stained a golden brown, it's difficult for anyone but a woodworker to tell the difference.

Cut the plywood sheets to the sizes you need for the case parts. Jim double-cut each sheet, sawing them into manageable sizes with a circular saw, then trimming them to final size on a table saw.

Plane the lumber to ¾ inch thick for the face frame members and ¼ inch thick for the trim. You can save a great deal of lumber by *resawing* 4/4 stock in half on a band saw, then planing the resawed boards to ¼ inch thick.

ANOTHER WAY TO GO ■ *Frame-and-Panel Construction*

You don't have to make the imitation frames and panels that Jim and I created by gluing thin strips to plywood sheets. We chose this particular method because we knew it would be easier for novice woodworkers. However, it requires more lumber and results in a heavier case than frame-and-panel construction.

If you'd rather stick to traditional methods, make the frame members from ¾-inch-thick stock. Cut grooves to hold ¼-inch plywood panels in all the *inside* edges. Cut tongues to fit the grooves where the end of one frame member joins the edge of another. When assembling the frames and panels, glue the frame members together, but let the panels "float" in their grooves.

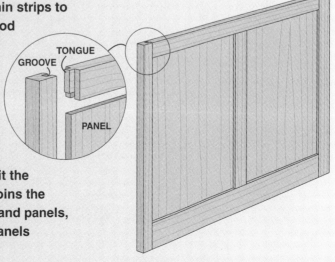

GROOVE TONGUE PANEL

MAKING THE JOINERY

As designed, the pedestals require little joinery. Cut rabbets in the back edges of the sides for the back. Make dadoes in the sides and the back to hold the top and bottom. Finally, rout a groove in the top to guide the pull-out shelf.

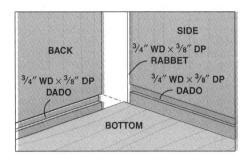

BACK

SIDE

³/₄″ WD × ³/₈″ DP RABBET

³/₄″ WD × ³/₈″ DP DADO

³/₄″ WD × ³/₈″ DP DADO

BOTTOM

Look Here! For more information on cutting rabbets and dadoes, see page 13.

Look Here! For more information on cutting rabbets and dadoes, see page 13.

TRY THIS!

Plywood is normally ¹/₃₂ inch less thick than its nominal dimension. To get a good fit when using ³/₄-inch plywood, cut rabbets and dadoes ²³/₃₂ inch wide. There are special router bits available just for this.

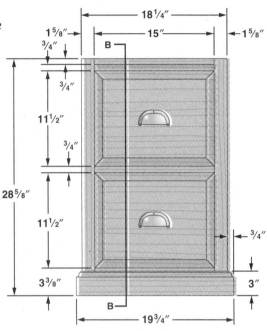

FRONT VIEW
WIDE PEDESTAL

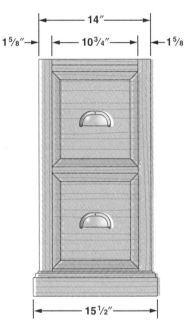

FRONT VIEW
NARROW PEDESTAL

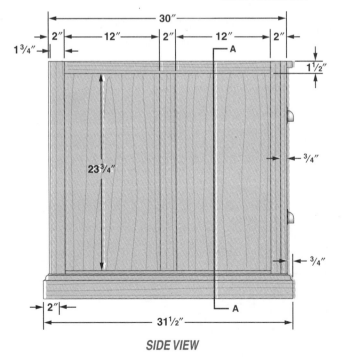

SIDE VIEW

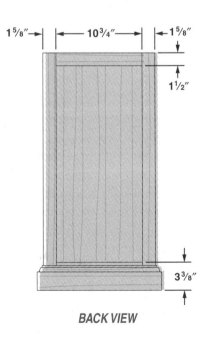

BACK VIEW

ASSEMBLING THE CASE Glue the plywood parts — sides, back, top, and bottom — together to form a large box, open at the front. Double-check that this assembly is square as you glue it up.

After the glue dries, apply the wood strips to the outside surfaces, creating frames on the sides and back. Because the cases are fairly large, Jim found it difficult to clamp the strips to the plywood parts while the glue dried. To solve this problem, he used a fast-drying wood molding glue (also called craft glue) to attach the strips. This glue develops "tack" quickly, holding the parts in place after just a few minutes of pressure.

Look Here! For more information on squaring a case, see page 33.

MAKING THE FACE FRAME Make a frame to cover the front edges of each pedestal case. The configuration of the face frame will depend not only on the size of the pedestal but also on the number and size of the drawers. Note that each drawer is divided from the others by a ¾-inch-wide rail. All the rails, in fact, are ¾ inch wide, including the bottom rail. Note that the bottom rail must be positioned so the base molding covers it just partway, leaving ⅜ inch showing.

Jim joined the rails to the stiles with glue and pocket screws. However, you can also use dowel joints.

NO PROBLEM

You glue two parts together, arrange the clamps, and as you're applying pressure, the parts slip out of position. No problem. Before you put the parts together, rub two pieces of 50-grit sandpaper together above the boards, knocking a few grains of sanding grit into the wet glue. When you put the parts together, the grit will keep the parts from slipping.

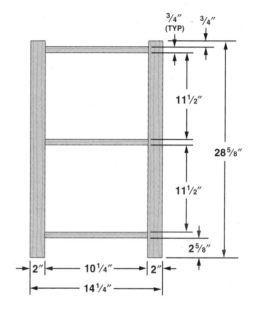

FACE FRAME LAYOUT

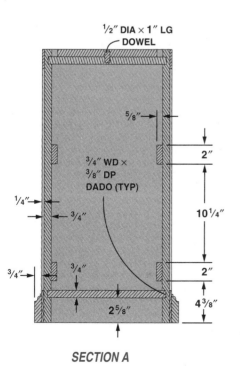

SECTION A

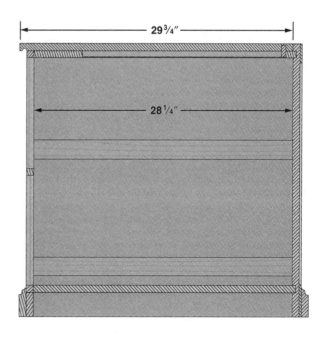

SECTION B

ATTACHING THE BASE MOLDING The base molding fits around the bottom of the case, making the pedestal look more solid and substantial. It's a simple molding to make — just rout an ogee shape in the top edge, as shown in the *Base Molding Profile*. You might also cut a cove or a bead, or make something more complex if that suits you.

Cut the molding stock to fit around the base of each pedestal, mitering the adjoining corners. Then glue it to the case.

FITTING THE PULLOUT SHELF The pullout shelf rests between the top of the case and the desktop, protruding about ¾ inch at the front. As you pull it out, a dowel in the underside of the shelf tracks the slot in the top, stopping the shelf when it's extended about 24 inches.

If you make this piece from solid wood, use quartersawn stock. Plain-sawn lumber has a tendency to cup — if the shelf does not remain flat, it will wedge itself in the desk.

Jim made the shelves on this desk from plywood, edging the sides and front so you can't see the plies. The edging on the front of each shelf is 1½ inches wide to create the look of a traditional "breadboard" assembly. Jim attached the breadboard ends with biscuits; you can also use splines or dowels. In the bottom face of the breadboard end, he routed a round-bottom groove. This serves as a handhold to pull the shelf out of the case.

Note: When making filing cabinets, the pullout shelves are nice to have on a two-drawer unit. But they serve little or no purpose on taller cabinets. They're too far above the floor to be useful. Shorten the case by ¾ inch, eliminating the space for the shelf.

DESIGNING THE DRAWERS When you make the face frame, you must decide on the size and number of drawers in each pedestal. If you're building a filing cabinet (or a pedestal that is intended to hold files), this is pretty well decided for you. All the drawers must be the same size, about 11 inches tall and 12 inches wide on the inside. However, you may want to make several smaller drawers as well to hold office supplies. In the drawing to the right, the left-hand pedestal holds two file drawers, while the right-hand pedestal holds a single file drawer and two smaller drawers, each 5⅜ inches tall. Note that the drawers in both configurations are separated by ¾-inch-wide rails.

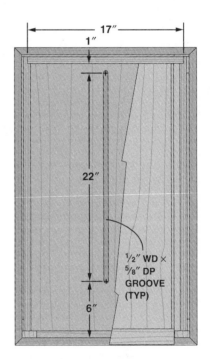

SECTION C

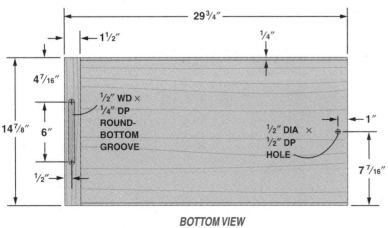

BOTTOM VIEW
PULLOUT SHELF LAYOUT

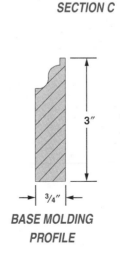

BASE MOLDING
PROFILE

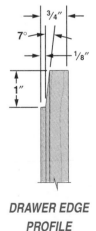

DRAWER EDGE
PROFILE

No matter what size you make the drawers, the construction is the same. Each drawer is a box, joined at the corners with half-blind dovetails. Jim attached decorative faces to the front of each drawer. The faces are beveled at the edges to form raised panels. Note that the face of each drawer is an inch wider than the drawer itself — it overhangs the drawer ½ inch on each side. This arrangement accommodates the extension slides and hides them when the drawer is closed.

The drawer face for the file drawer is also several inches taller than the drawer itself. As shown, the drawer is designed for hanging files and will accommodate a metal frame from which to hang them. (These are available at most office supply stores.) If you don't plan to hang the files, the front, back, and sides of the drawer should be almost as tall as the drawer face.

Note: Use quartersawn stock for the drawer faces. Plain-sawn stock may cup.

MAKING THE DRAWERS Before cutting the drawer parts, I make it a habit to carefully measure the drawer openings in the completed case and compare them to the dimensions on my plans. Cases, I've found, are always a fraction of an inch off the specs. This is normal; even if you cut and assemble all the parts precisely, the scraping and sanding you must do to smooth the wood surfaces will alter the dimension somewhat. Adjust the dimensions of the drawers to compensate for whatever discrepancies you find and cut the drawer parts to size.

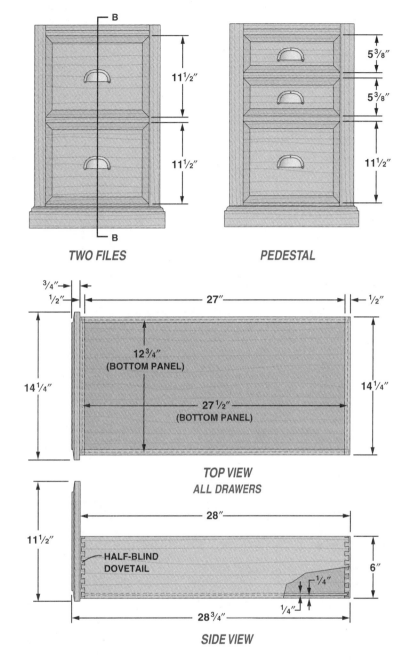

TWO FILES   **PEDESTAL**

TOP VIEW
ALL DRAWERS

HALF-BLIND DOVETAIL

SIDE VIEW

When designing the pedestals, remember to make room for the extension slides. Each slide is about ½ inch wide, so the drawer itself must be 1 inch narrower than the drawer opening. To hide the slides, make the drawer face almost the same size as the opening, or about 1 inch wider than the drawer.

The drawer bottoms rest in grooves. Rout these grooves in the inside faces of the front, back, and sides. Then rout the half-blind dovetails that join these parts. Jim assembled the front, back, and sides of each drawer with glue, but he let the drawer bottom "float" in the grooves, free to expand and contract.

Bevel all four edges of each drawer face, creating a raised panel. Then glue the panels to the drawer fronts. **Note: A *tall fence extension* and *guide strip* are invaluable aids when cutting raised panels.**

To make a raised panel, cut a steep bevel around the perimeter of a board. To make the step between the "field" and the bevels, position the fence so just the outside corners of the saw teeth break through the wood as you cut. Saw the ends first, then the edges. Clamp a guide strip to the panel so it rides along the top of the fence — this keeps the stock from dropping down onto the blade.

SHOP SAVVY

What's the proper way to orient the wood grain on the bottom of a drawer? The grain should run side to side. That way the drawer bottom will expand front to back, its least critical dimension. If it expands sideways, it could bow the sides, causing the drawer to stick.

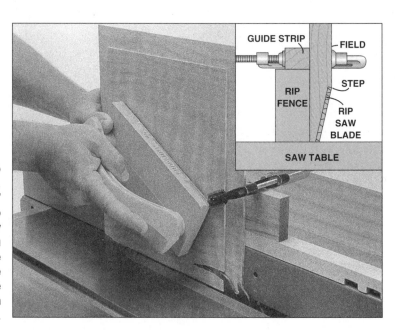

METHODS OF WORK ■ *Routing Half-Blind Dovetails*

Half-blind dovetails are the traditional choice for joining drawer parts, especially large drawers that see a lot of use. Because the tails and pins offer a lot of gluing surface, they're extremely strong when assembled. Additionally, they're easy to make with a router and a *dovetail jig*. Use a dovetail bit to cut the pins and tails, while following the template with a guide collar.

1 **To rout a half-blind dovetail,** secure both of the adjoining boards in a dovetail jig. The tail board is held vertically, its end flush with the top surface of the horizontal pin board. Cut both the tails and pins in one step, following the template with a guide collar.

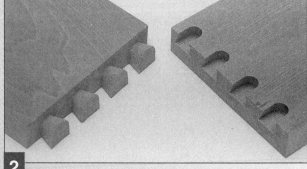

2 **The router cuts the tails** convex on the back side. These fit the concave slots between the pins, making a strong joint.

HANGING THE DRAWERS The drawers are suspended on full extension slides. These allow you to pull the drawer completely out of the case so you can reach all the files, even those way in the back.

Most extension slides come apart in two sections — the slide and the mount. The mount is attached to the drawer, while the slide itself is attached to the inside of the case. *However* (and this is an important however), the surface to which the slide is attached *must* be flush with the side of the drawer opening. That means that when you use this hardware on a traditional cabinet with a face frame, you can't attach the slide directly to the case. Attach a ⅝-inch-thick board (a *drawer mount*) to the side. When attached, the face of the mount should be flush with the opening. Then attach the slide to the mount. The drawer mounts are shown in *Section A* and *Section B*.

After mounting the slides inside the case, attach the mounts to the drawers. How do you align the two parts? Measure the distance to the centerline of the slide above the bottom edge of the drawer opening. Attach the mounts to the drawers that same distance *minus ¹⁄₁₆ inch* above the bottom edge of the drawer. (On this project, Jim mounted the slides 1 inch from the bottom edge of the drawer opening and ¹⁵⁄₁₆ inch from the bottom edge of the drawer.)

To hang the drawer, insert the mounts in the slides, then slide the drawer all the way into the case. Test the sliding action of the drawer. If it rubs or binds, don't panic. The screw holes on both the slides and the mounts are either elongated or slightly oversize. By loosening the screws that hold the hardware, you can adjust the position of the drawer up or down a fraction of an inch.

Hang the drawer so the bottom edge clears the drawer opening by about ¹⁄₁₆ inch.

EXTENSION SLIDE

DRAWER MOUNT

½" (TYP)

DRAWER SIDE

¹⁵⁄₁₆"

1"

¹⁄₁₆"

BOTTOM EDGE OF DRAWER OPENING

CONSIDER THIS

When hanging drawers, you may want to attach the drawer faces to the drawer fronts after hanging the drawers. Once the drawers are in place and working properly, adhere a few strips of double-faced carpet tape to the drawer front. Make sure the drawer face fits the opening with ¹⁄₃₂ to ¹⁄₁₆ to spare all around the perimeter. Position the drawer face where you want it and press the parts together. Check the action of the drawer. If the face rubs or binds, detach it and try again. When the face is positioned, drill two to four holes through the drawer front and into the back side of the face. Screw and glue the face to the front.

ANOTHER WAY TO GO ■ *Drawer Guides*

While extension slides are nice, they are also expensive. If you don't need to pull a drawer all the way out of your pedestal, consider making *drawer guides* instead. Glue strips of a very hard wood (such as oak or maple) to the drawer mounts, and cut grooves to fit the strips in the drawer sides. The grooves should be ¹⁄₃₂ to ¹⁄₁₆ inch wider and deeper than the strips to let the drawer slide smoothly. To make the drawer guides adjustable, drill oversize counterbored pilot holes in the drawer mounts and attach the mounts to the cabinet sides with screws.

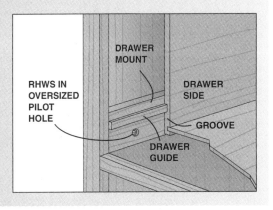

DRAWER MOUNT

RHWS IN OVERSIZED PILOT HOLE

DRAWER SIDE

GROOVE

DRAWER GUIDE

DESIGN SAVVY ■ *Cabinets for Computers*

The pedestal cabinet shown here will hold more than files and office supplies. With a little ingenuity, you can adapt one or more of the pedestals on your desk to hold computer components. Jim and I designed one of the pedestals on our desk to hold a computer CPU. To do this, we had to solve several problems.

To keep the CPU cool inside the enclosed pedestal, we drilled ventilation holes and installed a muffin fan on the *kneehole side* of the pedestal, where they wouldn't be too noticeable. They're almost completely hidden by the desktop. The dark "golden oak" stain that we used also helps to disguise them. I plugged the fan into the same power strip used to power up the computer, so the fan runs whenever the computer is on.

Which brings me to the second problem. How do you get the wires in and out of the pedestal unobtrusively? Some wires, such as power cords and modem lines, needed to exit near the bottom of the pedestal. Others, such as the monitor and printer cables, needed to exit near the top. Additionally, some of the connectors on these cables were fairly large. For example, the DB25 connector on the end of a standard printer cable is over 3 inches wide. How do you dress up a hole that wide in a pedestal with wires leaking out of it?

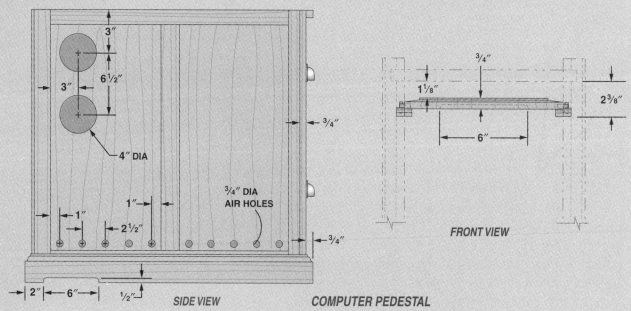

SIDE VIEW   COMPUTER PEDESTAL   FRONT VIEW

For the wires that we needed to run from the bottom of the pedestal, we drilled a 4-inch-diameter hole in the bottom shelf, then cut a shallow relief in the bottom edge of the base molding (as shown in the *Computer Pedestal/Side View*). With this arrangement, the large hole doesn't show at all, and the relief is barely visible, especially if the pedestal rests on a carpet.

For the wires that we needed to run toward the top, we cut a 4-inch-diameter hole in the kneehole side (you could also make it in the back), then fashioned a cover, as shown in the *Cable Opening Cover*. We fastened the cover in place with two turnbuttons to partially disguise the hole (or, at least give it a more finished appearance) after running the wires through it.

We also modified the front of the cabinet, making a door to hide the computer when it's not in use. The door is a piece of plywood, edged in hardwood, with thin strips and panels glued to it to look like a set of drawers. It also *disappears* back into the case when you open it. (We didn't want the door hanging open, banging your knees every time you leave your desk.) For this we designed a mechanism similar to that used for the doors in a

"barrister's bookcase." The upper part of the door is hung on two steel pins, one on each side. The pins rest in slots in the face frame stiles, as shown in the *Stile Slot Detail*. When you open the door, the pins slide back along two brackets until they are stopped by two more steel pins at the back of the brackets. Make the brackets from a very hard wood, such as maple or oak. To prevent the door from swinging on the pins when it's closed, install two bullet catches, one on either side, near the bottom of the door. *Don't use magnetic catches!* Magnets may corrupt the data on computer disks.

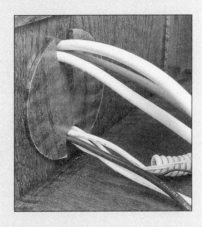

After running the wires that go to the desktop, insert the cable opening cover in the pedestal, and rotate the turnbuttons to secure it. This not only dresses up the hole but it also helps to hold the cables in place.

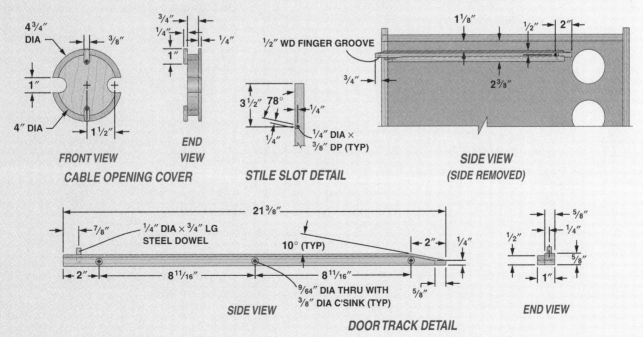

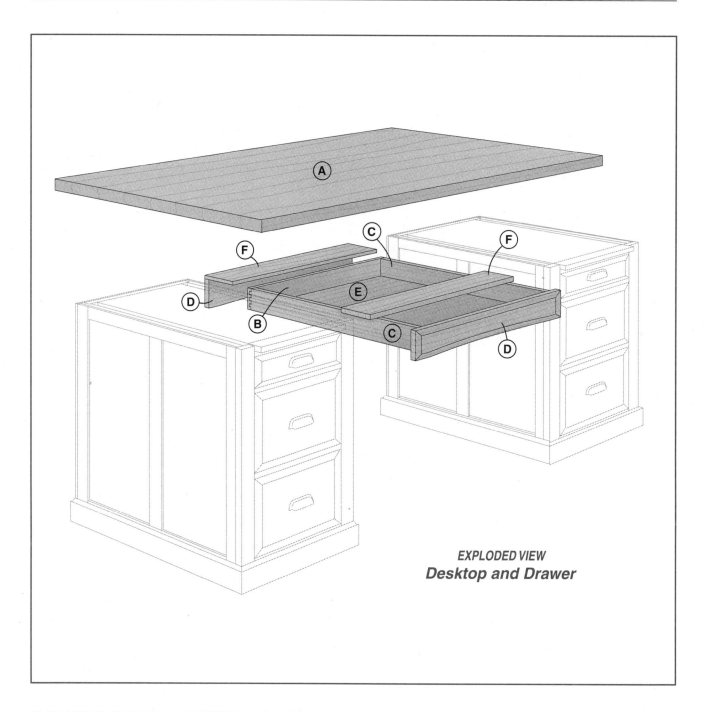

EXPLODED VIEW
Desktop and Drawer

ROLLTOP DESK ■ *MATERIALS LIST* (Finished Dimensions)

PARTS — DESKTOP AND DRAWER

A	Desktop	$1\frac{3}{8}$″ × 32″ × (variable)
B	Drawer front/back (2)	$\frac{1}{2}$″ × 3″ × 21″
C	Drawer sides (2)	$\frac{1}{2}$″ × 3″ × $26\frac{3}{4}$″
D	Drawer face/back apron	$\frac{3}{4}$″ × 4″ × 22″
E	Drawer bottom*	$\frac{1}{4}$″ × $20\frac{1}{2}$″ × $26\frac{1}{2}$″
F	Pedestal ties (2)	$\frac{3}{4}$″ × 4″ × 22″

HARDWARE

$\frac{1}{4}$″ Cross dowels and bolts (9)

24″ Extension slides and mounting screws (2)

$\frac{1}{4}$″ × $2\frac{1}{2}$″ Roundhead stove bolts (8)

Tabletop fasteners and mounting screws (8)

$\frac{1}{4}$″ Square nuts (8)

$\frac{1}{4}$″ Flat washers (8)

Make this part from plywood.

If you have decided to make filing cabinets, you'll need to add a top to each case. If you plan to make a desk, the next step is to join the pedestals and add a desktop and a drawer

MAKING A PEDESTAL DESK

The pedestal desk consists of four components, two of which — the pedestals — you've already made. Next, you'll need to make a middle drawer to suspend between the pedestals and a desktop to rest across the pedestals.

PREPARING THE MATERIALS Decide how you are going to make the top. There are three methods you can use.

■ Glue up a solid wood slab, 1⅜ inches thick, by joining thick boards edge to edge. If you join wide, plain-sawn boards, turn them so the heartwood faces up. For narrower quartersawn stock, turn the boards so the annual rings run top to bottom. This "butcherblock" configuration is the most stable option for thick slabs — it expands and contracts less and has little tendency to warp or cup.

■ Glue up a solid wood slab from ¾-inch-thick boards, orienting them so the heartwood faces up. Trim the slab with 1⅜-inch-wide banding all around the perimeter to make it appear thicker.

■ Make a "torsion box" top. This is essentially two thin pieces of plywood (the "skin" of the box), sandwiched to wooden framework. This is the lightest of the three alternatives, the most stable, and the least likely to warp or cup.

Jim and I used the third alternative (the torsion box), but we didn't make it from scratch. Instead, we bought a hollow-core oak-veneer interior door, 32 inches wide, and cut it to the length needed. Jim glued a rib in the open (cut) end, then banded the edges of the door with solid oak strips. The finished desktop looks great, and it saved us some money.

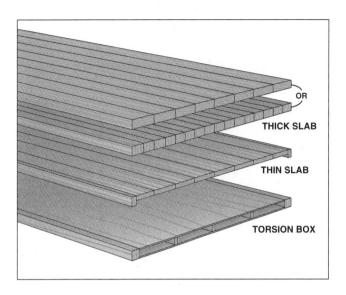

THICK SLAB

THIN SLAB

TORSION BOX

The only drawback Jim found was that the veneer on the interior door was extremely thin, and it took some finesse to sand the banding flush to the surface of the door without going through the veneer.

JOINING THE PEDESTALS For the drawer to work properly, the pedestals must remain parallel to one another and a constant distance apart. To hold them in place, Jim joined them with two pedestal ties.

Drill 1-inch-diameter holes near the ends of the pedestal ties, as shown in the *Pedestal Tie Joinery Detail*. Also drill ¼-inch-diameter holes through the tie ends and matching holes in the kneehole sides of the pedestals.

TRY THIS!

To keep from cutting through the veneer when banding a plywood edge, cut the bands slightly wider than needed. Apply them to the assembly so the banding is slightly proud of the veneer surface. Draw a pencil mark on the veneer next to the band, then scrape or sand the edge of the banding until you just begin to remove the mark. Stop when you see the mark beginning to disappear.

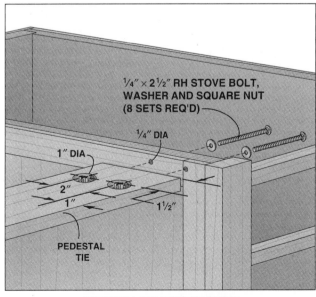

¼″ × 2½″ RH STOVE BOLT, WASHER AND SQUARE NUT (8 SETS REQ'D)

¼″ DIA

1″ DIA

2″

1″

1½″

PEDESTAL TIE

PEDESTAL TIE JOINERY DETAIL

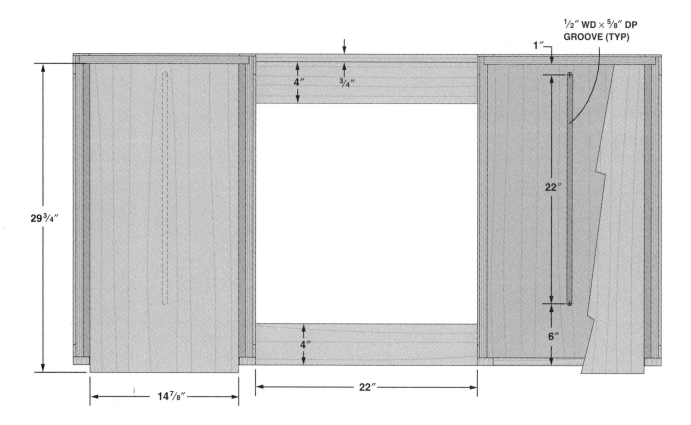

JOINING THE PEDESTALS

Using a band saw, cut the shape of the back apron and the middle drawer face, as shown in the *Drawer Front and Back Apron Layout.* Sand the sawed edges. Set the drawer face aside for the time being, but glue the back apron to the back pedestal tie, forming an L-shaped beam.

Attach the ties to the pedestals with roundhead stove bolts and nuts. When assembled, the top faces of the ties should be flush with the top edges of the pedestals. The edge of the front tie and the face of the back apron should be even with the front and back surfaces of the pedestals.

ATTACHING THE TOP Jim decided to hold the desktop in place with tabletop fasteners, small metal gussets that look like a figure 8. Attach the fasteners to the top edges of the pedestals, driving the screw down into the sides. Position the desktop on the desk and drive the screws up through the fasteners and into the top.

For the top to sit solidly on the pedestal, the fasteners must be mortised into either the top edges of the pedestals or the underside of the desktop.

Ordinarily, woodworkers choose the first option, routing out the mortises in the pedestals with a hand-held router and a straight bit.

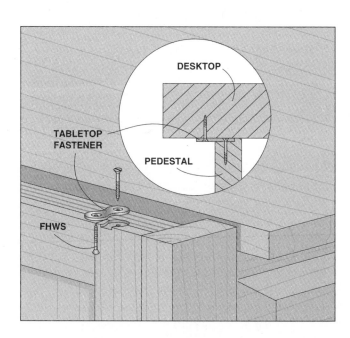

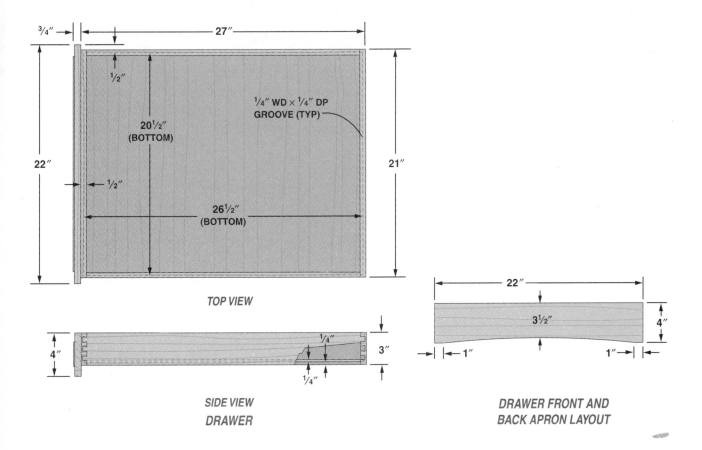

TOP VIEW

SIDE VIEW
DRAWER

DRAWER FRONT AND
BACK APRON LAYOUT

Note: If you're making filing cabinets, make tops to cover the individual cases with a 1-inch overhang all around. Fasten them to the cases in exactly the same manner, using tabletop fasteners.

To rout a mortise for a tabletop fastener, trace the outline of the fastener on the top edge of the pedestal. Lay the slide-out shelf on the top shelf to create a wide surface to support the router, and rout out the waste. The completed mortise must be as deep as the fastener is thick.

MAKING THE DRAWER The drawer between the pedestals is shallower and wider than those in the pedestals, but the construction is almost exactly the same. Jim joined the sides to the front and back with half-blind dovetails, then glued the drawer face on the drawer front. The drawer bottom rests in grooves in the front, back, and sides.

There is one important difference, however. When you apply the faces to the drawers in the pedestal, the bottom edges of the faces must be flush with the bottom edges of the fronts. On the middle drawer, it's just the other way around — the top edges must be flush, as shown in the *Drawer/Side View.*

Look Here! For more information on making half-blind dovetails, see page 62.

HANGING THE DRAWER Hang the middle drawer between the two pedestals so the top edge of the drawer just clears the ties. Jim suspended this drawer on extension sides, using the same hardware he used to hang the drawers in the pedestals. Attach the slides to the kneehole sides of the pedestal and the mounts to the sides of the drawer. This time, measure the position of the slides and mounts from the top. Attach the slides to the pedestals 1 inch below the bottom surfaces of the pedestal ties, and to the drawers $1\frac{1}{16}$ inch below the top edges of the sides. Remember to drive the screws through the elongated or oversize holes in the hardware. This enables you to adjust the position of the drawer slightly after it's hung.

Note: You don't need to go to the expense of full extension slides for this drawer. It will likely be used to store small items such as pens and pencils. You shouldn't need to pull it all the way out of the desk. In fact, this may prove awkward when you're seated at the desk. A slide that offers two-thirds extension will do just fine.

SHOP SAVVY

Extension slides offer a quick, simple method for hanging drawers, but there are some tricks you need to know to install them properly.

■ Position the front end of each slide where you want the *back* surface of the drawer face to stop when you push the drawer into the case. For example, if the drawer face is ¾ inch thick and you want the face to be flush with the outside of the case, place the slide ¾ inch in from the front of the case.

■ Take care that the slides are perfectly parallel, or the drawer will bind. If the drawer seems to fit its opening properly, but doesn't slide smoothly, chances are the slides are not parallel and must be adjusted.

■ To adjust the position of a slide, loosen the screws that hold it in place. The screws should be snug, but not tight. Tap the slide up or down and test the drawer action. When the drawer is working properly, tighten the screws.

ANOTHER WAY TO GO ■ *Drawer Brackets*

Instead of slides, consider hanging the middle drawer on *drawer brackets* —long, wooden L-shaped assemblies. Attach the brackets to the kneehole sides of the pedestals so the drawer is cradled between them. To keep the drawer from tipping forward when you pull it out, attach turnbuttons to the back of the drawer. When turned vertically, the top ends of the turnbuttons should almost touch the underside of the desktop. The turnbuttons also prevent you from accidentally pulling the drawer all the way out of the case.

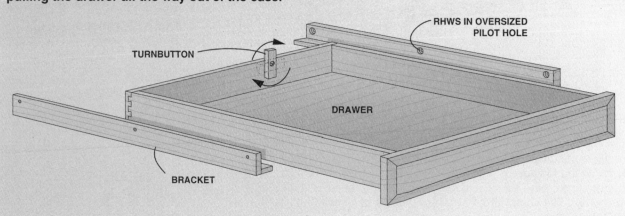

TURNBUTTON

RHWS IN OVERSIZED PILOT HOLE

DRAWER

BRACKET

QUICK FIXTURE ■ *Extension Slide Drill Guide*

If you install several extension slides, all the same length, it will pay you to make some simple drill guides to help shoot the pilot holes. These will help you position the holes accurately and keep the slides and mounts parallel.

You will need to make two guides, one for drilling the pilot holes to attach the slides and another for the mounts. Remember to take into account the vertical position of the drawer mounts in relation to the drawer openings. In our desk, the mounts are 1 inch above the bottom of the openings. Use the hardware itself as a template. First, scribe a line along the face of a 3-inch-wide strip of ¼-inch plywood, 1¼ inch from one edge. Take an extension apart and align the slides so the holes are over the line you just made. Make sure the front end of the slide is flush with the end of the board, then mark the locations of the holes. *Also mark the front end of the board!* Repeat for the mount, but scribe the line 2³⁄₁₆ inch from the edge of the board. Drill holes at the marks the same diameter as the pilot holes you plan to make.

Cut ¼-inch-wide, ¼-inch-deep grooves in the cleats and glue them to the edge of the guides.

When assembled, the holes in the slide drill guide should be 1 inch from the face of the cleat. The holes in the mount drilling guide should be 1¹⁵⁄₁₆ inches from the cleat.

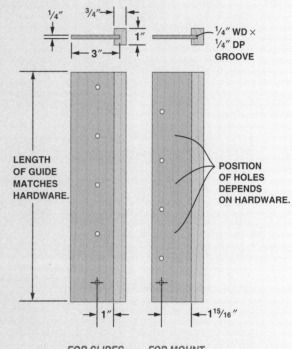

LENGTH OF GUIDE MATCHES HARDWARE.

POSITION OF HOLES DEPENDS ON HARDWARE.

¼" WD × ¼" DP GROOVE

FOR SLIDES   FOR MOUNT

DRILLING GUIDES

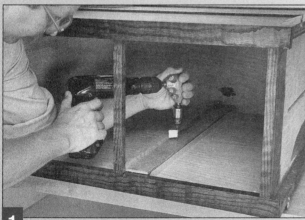

1 **To use the guides,** hook the cleat of the slide guide over the bottom edge of the drawer mount. Make sure the front of the guide is facing forward. Clamp the guide in place (or hold it with double-faced carpet tape) and drill the pilot holes. Repeat this procedure with the mount guide, hooking the cleat over the bottom edge of the drawer side.

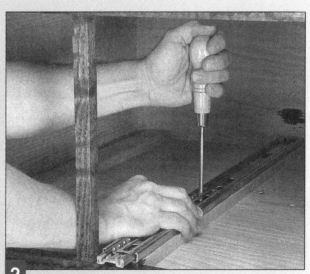

2 **After drilling the pilot holes,** screw the hardware to the drawer mounts and the drawers. Then attach the drawers to the slides. If necessary, adjust the position of the slides and the mounts by loosening the screws.

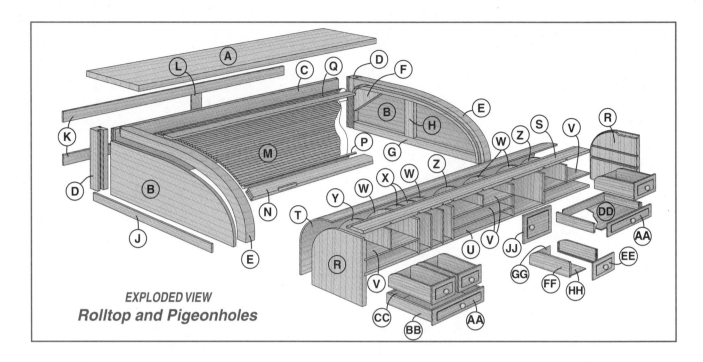

EXPLODED VIEW
Rolltop and Pigeonholes

ROLLTOP DESK ■ *MATERIALS LIST* (Finished Dimensions)

PARTS — ROLLTOP AND PIGEONHOLES

A	Top	$1\frac{1}{4}'' \times 13\frac{1}{4}'' \times$ (variable)
B	Sides* (2)	$\frac{3}{4}'' \times 11\frac{3}{8}'' \times 27\frac{3}{4}''$
C	Back*	$\frac{3}{4}'' \times 12\frac{3}{4}'' \times$ (variable)
D	Corner stiles (2)	$1\frac{3}{4}'' \times 1\frac{3}{4}'' \times 12\frac{3}{4}''$
E	Curved rails (2)	$1\frac{3}{4}'' \times 8\frac{1}{4}'' \times 32''$
F	Corner blocks (2)	$\frac{3}{4}'' \times 5'' \times 5''$
G	Inside trim rails (2)	$\frac{3}{4}'' \times 1\frac{3}{4}'' \times 27''$
H	Inside trim stiles (2)	$\frac{3}{4}'' \times 1\frac{3}{4}'' \times 9\frac{1}{4}''$
J	Outside side trim rails (2)	$\frac{1}{4}'' \times 1\frac{3}{4}'' \times 27''$
K	Outside back trim rails (2)	$\frac{1}{4}'' \times 1\frac{3}{4}'' \times$ (variable)
L	Outside back trim stile	$\frac{1}{4}'' \times 1\frac{3}{4}'' \times 9\frac{1}{4}''$
M	Tambours (35)	$\frac{3}{8}'' \times \frac{5}{8}'' \times$ (variable)
N	Tambour lead	$\frac{3}{4}'' \times 2'' \times$ (variable)
P	Tambour attachment strip	$\frac{5}{16}'' \times \frac{5}{16}'' \times$ (variable)
Q	Top spacer	$\frac{5}{8}'' \times 2'' \times$ (variable)
R	Pigeonhole sides (2)	$\frac{3}{4}'' \times 9\frac{1}{2}'' \times 11\frac{1}{2}''$
S	Pigeonhole top	$\frac{1}{2}'' \times 3'' \times$ (variable)
T	Pigeonhole back*	$\frac{1}{4}'' \times 16\frac{7}{8}'' \times$ (variable)
U	Pigeonhole bottom shelf	$\frac{1}{2}'' \times 9\frac{1}{4}'' \times$ (variable)
V	Pigeonhole middle shelves (4)	$\frac{1}{4}'' \times 9\frac{1}{4}'' \times$ (variable)
W	Pigeonhole dividers (4)	$\frac{1}{2}'' \times 9\frac{1}{4}'' \times 5\frac{7}{8}''$
X	Pigeonhole letter dividers (2)	$\frac{1}{4}'' \times 9\frac{1}{4}'' \times 5\frac{7}{8}''$
Y	Pigeonhole top drawer dividers (2)	$\frac{1}{4}'' \times 9\frac{1}{8}'' \times 3\frac{1}{2}''$
Z	Center divider	$\frac{1}{4}'' \times 2'' \times 9\frac{1}{4}''$
AA	Large drawer faces (2)	$\frac{1}{2}'' \times 2\frac{3}{16}'' \times$ (variable)
BB	Large drawer sides (4)	$\frac{1}{4}'' \times 1\frac{15}{16}'' \times 9''$
CC	Large drawer backs (2)	$\frac{1}{4}'' \times 1\frac{7}{16}'' \times$ (variable)
DD	Large drawer bottoms* (2)	$\frac{1}{4}'' \times 8\frac{15}{16}'' \times$ (variable)
EE	Small drawer faces (4)	$\frac{1}{2}'' \times 3\frac{5}{16}'' \times$ (variable)
FF	Small drawer sides (8)	$\frac{1}{4}'' \times 3\frac{1}{16}'' \times 9''$
GG	Small drawer backs (4)	$\frac{1}{4}'' \times 1\frac{3}{4}'' \times$ (variable)
HH	Small drawer bottoms* (4)	$\frac{1}{4}'' \times 8\frac{15}{16}'' \times$ (variable)
JJ	Compartment door	$\frac{1}{2}'' \times 5\frac{5}{8}'' \times$ (variable)

Make these parts from plywood.

HARDWARE

Heavy canvas 26″ × (variable)

½″ Drawer pulls (6)

Surface-mounted cupboard lock

Escutcheon

⅜″ × 1½″ Dowels (6)

#10 × 2½″ Flathead wood screws (6)

#8 × 1½″ Flathead wood screws (2)

1″ Wire brads (20–24)

RESOURCES

If you wish, you can purchase a sheet of tambours
already glued to a canvas backing from:
    Rockler Woodworking and Hardware
    4365 Willow Drive
    Medina, MN 55340

The rolltop attaches to the top of the pedestal desk,
transforming it into a rolltop desk. This is actually a
cabinet with a sliding tambour door.

MAKING THE ROLLTOP

As with any cabinet, it's best to make the case first,
then fit the inserts to it. In this case the inserts are
the pigeonholes and the pigeonhole drawers.

PREPARING THE MATERIALS The dimensions
shown in the drawing presume that you are
building a desk with a top 52½ inches from side
to side. If the top on your desk is longer, subtract
52½ from the actual length, then add the result to
all the dimensions in the drawings that are marked
"variable" on the Materials List. If the top is shorter,
subtract the actual length from 52½, then subtract
that result from the variable dimensions.

Purchase 8/4 (2-inch-thick) stock to make the
top, the corner stiles, and the curved rails. The rest
of the parts can be made from 4/4 (1-inch-thick)
stock. You'll also need ¾-inch plywood for the back
and sides, and ¼-inch plywood for the drawer
bottoms.

Plane the solid wood to the thickness you need.
When making ¼- and ⅜-inch-thick stock for some
of the pigeonhole and pigeonhole drawer parts,
remember that you can save lumber by *resawing*
the 4/4 stock in half before you plane it to its final
dimension.

If necessary, glue up wide stock for the top and
the curved rails. Then cut all the case parts to the
proper length and width. For now, set the pigeonhole and pigeonhole drawer stock aside.

CUTTING THE CURVED RAILS Lay out the shapes
of the curved rails, as shown in the *Curved Rail
Layout.* You can enlarge the grid on the drawing,
but you'll get more accurate results if you construct
the shape of the rail with a little draftsmanship. The
area marked "A" on the drawing is a rectangular
shape, 1¾ inches by 11 inches. Area C is a square,
1¾ inches by 1¾ inches. Area B is one quarter of an
oval. The outside curve has a major axis (length) of
36 inches and a minor axis (width) of 22 inches. For

SHOP SAVVY ■ *Laying Out an Oval*

To draw an accurate oval or elliptical curve, you must know its length and width.
The length is called the major axis, and the width is the minor axis.

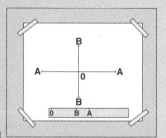

1 Draw the major (A-A) and
minor (B-B) axes perpendicular to
one another so they cross at their
midpoints (0). On a straightedge,
mark the lengths 0A and 0B (half
of the major and minor axes).

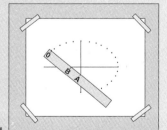

2 Place the straightedge so the
A mark falls on the minor axis and
the B mark on the major axis. Make a
mark at 0. Change the straightedge
angle, realign the marks with the
axes, and make another dot.

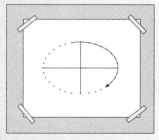

3 Repeat until you have
drawn as much of the ellipse as
needed, then connect the dots to
form a curve. **Tip: By making a
quarter oval template, then
turning it this way and that, you
can lay out both partial and
complete ellipses.**

the inside curve, subtract 3½ inches from the major and minor axes to make an elliptical curve 32½ inches by 18½ inches.

Also cut the shapes of the sides. The elliptical curve on these parts is 33¼ inches by 19¼ inches. Cut the curved parts with a band saw and sand the sawed surfaces.

MAKING THE JOINERY After cutting the case parts to size and shape, make the joinery. There's a lot of joinery in this assembly, but it's all pretty simple. Cut:

■ ¾-inch-wide, ⅜-inch-deep grooves on the inside faces of the corner stiles that join the sides, as shown in *Section B*

■ ¾-inch-wide, ⅜-inch-deep grooves in the inside faces of the curved stiles, as shown in *Section C*

■ ⅜-inch-wide, ⅜-inch-deep grooves in the inside surfaces of the corner stiles that join the back

■ ⅜-inch-wide, ⅜-inch-deep rabbets in the left and right edges of the back, forming tenons to fit the grooves in the corner stiles

■ ¾-inch-wide, ⅜-inch-long tenons on the back ends of the curved rails, as shown in the *Curved Rail Tenon Detail*

Rout the grooves for the sides in the inside surfaces of the curved rails with a slot cutter. Make several passes, adjusting the height of the cutter with each pass, to cut the full ¾-inch-wide groove.

Cut the tenon in the back ends of the curved rails on a table saw, using a dado cutter. Place the long, straight section of the rail against a miter gauge to guide the rail over the cutter.

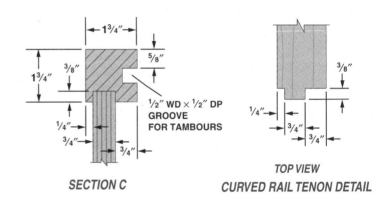

SECTION C   TOP VIEW
CURVED RAIL TENON DETAIL

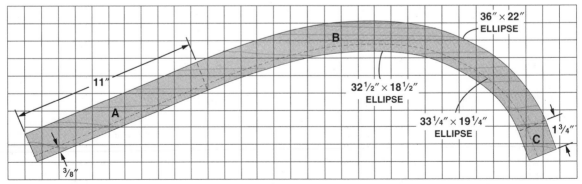

1 SQUARE = 1″

CURVED RAIL LAYOUT

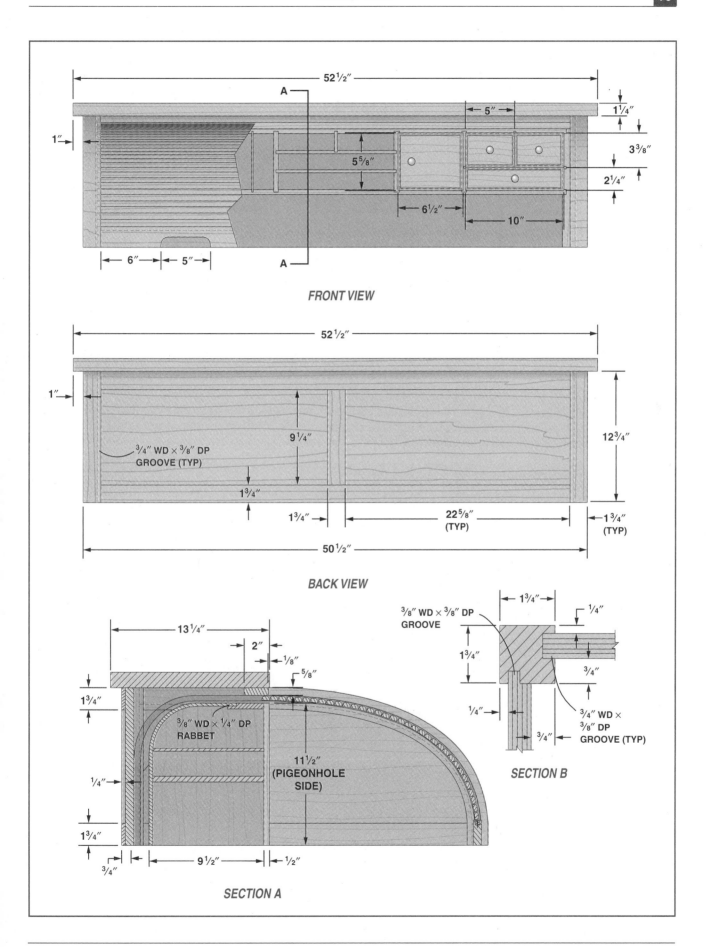

FRONT VIEW

BACK VIEW

SECTION A

SECTION B

ASSEMBLE THE SIDES Do not cut the grooves for the tambour just yet. Because these grooves pass through several parts, it's best to make them *after* the sides are assembled.

Glue the sides, corner stiles, and curved rails together. When the glue sets up, add the corner blocks, inside trim, and outside trim, gluing these pieces to the inside faces of the side. **Note: The two side assemblies should be mirror images of one another.**

CUTTING THE TAMBOUR GROOVES The grooves for the tambour run parallel to the curve of the curved rails, turn a radius through the corner block, and run straight down the corner stiles. To cut these grooves, you must do a little *pattern routing*. Make a template for the inside edge of the groove, then use the template to guide your router and a pattern routing bit.

Make 1½-inch-thick stock for the template by laminating two ¾-inch sheets of plywood or particleboard face to face. Lay out the template on the stock. The elliptical curve at the front of the groove has a major axis of 33¾ inches and a minor axis of 19¾ inches. The curve at the back is a section of a circle with a radius of 4½ inches. Cut the template with a band saw or saber saw, cutting a little wide of the layout line. Sand the cut edges smooth, sanding down to the line.

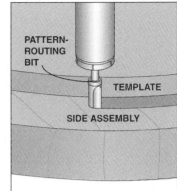

Create the groove for the tambour with a ½-inch pattern-routing bit. As you rout, guide the pilot bearing on the bit along the edge of a template.

Adhere the template to the inside surface of a side assembly with double-faced carpet tape. Make absolutely certain that the curve of the template is parallel to the curve of the ellipse. The front edge of the template should be 1⅛ inches from the front edge of the side assembly, and the template back edge 1 inch from the assembly back edge.

Adjust the router to cut just 1⁄16 inch deep into the side assembly. Rest the base of the router on the template and press the bearing on the pattern routing bit firmly against the template. Rout a shallow groove, keeping the bit against the template as you cut. Make several passes, cutting just 1⁄16 inch deeper with each pass until the groove is ½ inch deep. Repeat the sequence on the second side.

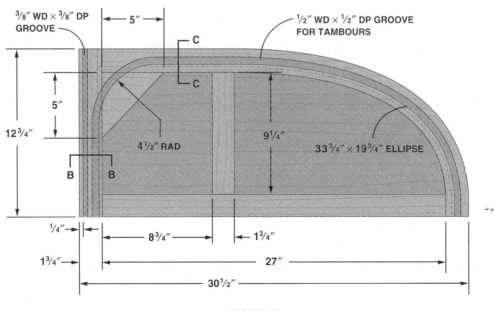

INSIDE VIEW
ASSEMBLED SIDE PANEL

MAKING THE TAMBOURS Pick a board with the straightest grain you can find and plane it to ⅝-inch thick. Joint both edges, then round all the arrises with a ¼-inch roundover bit and a router. Cut a ⅜-inch-wide strip from each edge, then repeat until you have made all the tambour strips you need. (Actually, Jim and I have found that it's best to make more than you need and keep only the ones that turn out reasonably straight.) Glue the strips to a canvas backing, leaving a little 1-inch-wide strip of canvas showing on one edge.

Cut the tambour lead board, cutting tenons in the ends and stopped rabbets in the bottom edge, as shown in the *Tambour Lead Board Layout*. The rabbets serve as handholds when you open the rolltop. Also cut a ⅜-inch-wide, ⅜-inch-deep groove in the top edge of the board. To attach the tambours to the lead board, press the canvas tab into the groove with a slender wooden attachment strip; then fasten the strip with flathead wood screws.

NO PROBLEM

You lay out the grooves for the tambour in large, gentle arcs, cut them smooth and precise, make the tambours from the straightest of woods, but still the tambours bind in their grooves.

No problem. Remove the tambours and inspect the sides of the grooves for splinters and rough spots. If you find none, you may need to attach a counterweight to the inside edge of the tambour door. Using short lengths of wire, attach a length of iron pipe to the last tambour. This will help pull the door open as you push on the lead board. Note: If you need less weight, reduce the length of pipe. For more weight, use a longer pipe or a solid iron bar.

½" I.D. PIPE

WIRE

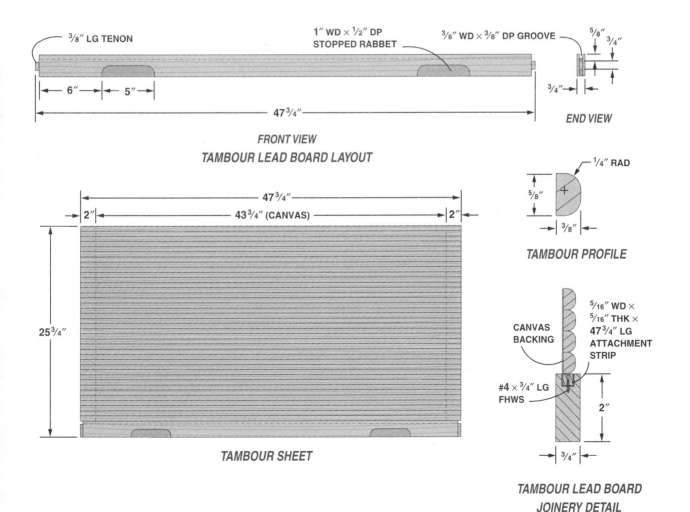

⅜" LG TENON

1" WD × ½" DP STOPPED RABBET

⅜" WD × ⅜" DP GROOVE

⅝" ¾"

6"   5"

47¾"

¾"

END VIEW

FRONT VIEW
TAMBOUR LEAD BOARD LAYOUT

47¾"

2"   43¾" (CANVAS)   2"

25¾"

TAMBOUR SHEET

¼" RAD

⅝"

⅜"

TAMBOUR PROFILE

⁵⁄₁₆" WD × ⁵⁄₁₆" THK × 47¾" LG ATTACHMENT STRIP

CANVAS BACKING

#4 × ¾" LG FHWS

2"

¾"

TAMBOUR LEAD BOARD JOINERY DETAIL

SHOP SAVVY ■ *Designing and Assembling Tamboured Doors*

Tamboured doors work well on desks for several reasons. Unlike a hinged door, it doesn't swing out. Consequently, you don't have to move things on your desk. And unlike a sliding door, which leaves a portion of the space behind it covered, the tamboured door provides unobstructed access when open.

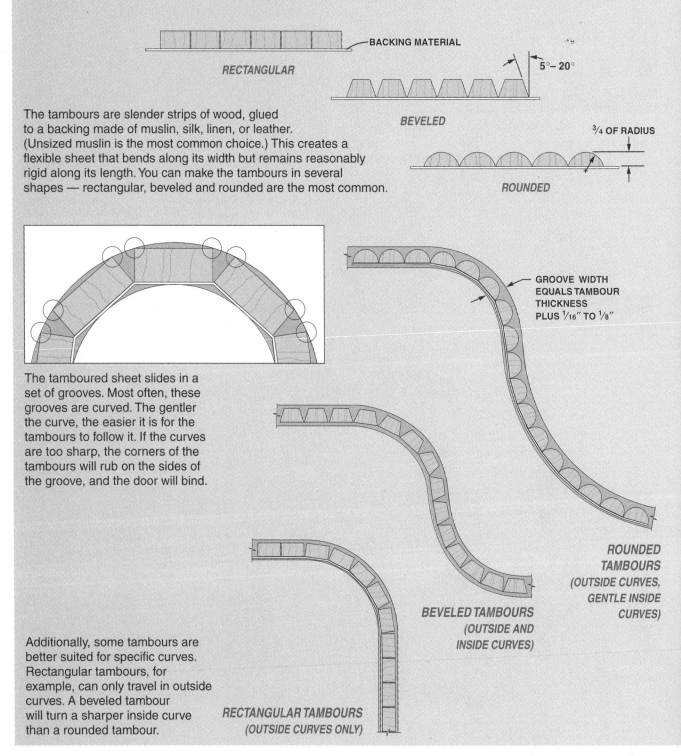

RECTANGULAR

BACKING MATERIAL

5°– 20°

BEVELED

¾ OF RADIUS

ROUNDED

The tambours are slender strips of wood, glued to a backing made of muslin, silk, linen, or leather. (Unsized muslin is the most common choice.) This creates a flexible sheet that bends along its width but remains reasonably rigid along its length. You can make the tambours in several shapes — rectangular, beveled and rounded are the most common.

GROOVE WIDTH EQUALS TAMBOUR THICKNESS PLUS ¹⁄₁₆″ TO ¹⁄₈″

The tamboured sheet slides in a set of grooves. Most often, these grooves are curved. The gentler the curve, the easier it is for the tambours to follow it. If the curves are too sharp, the corners of the tambours will rub on the sides of the groove, and the door will bind.

ROUNDED TAMBOURS (OUTSIDE CURVES, GENTLE INSIDE CURVES)

BEVELED TAMBOURS (OUTSIDE AND INSIDE CURVES)

Additionally, some tambours are better suited for specific curves. Rectangular tambours, for example, can only travel in outside curves. A beveled tambour will turn a sharper inside curve than a rounded tambour.

RECTANGULAR TAMBOURS (OUTSIDE CURVES ONLY)

To assemble the tambours, make a simple jig to hold them edge to edge while you apply the backing. Load the tambours in the jig, back side up. Gently squeeze them together with wedges to straighten any slightly curved tambours. Cut the backing 4 inches narrower than the tambours are long.

Mask off 1 to 2 inches of the backing material along the edge where you will later attach the lead board. Apply a thin, even coating of white or yellow glue to the backing. With a helper, peel up the backing, turn it glue side down, and position it on the tambours, letting the masked portion overhang the first tambour. Carefully spread the backing so there are no wrinkles, trim the edges straight with a razor or a sharp knife, and let the glue dry. **Caution: Don't apply glue directly to the tambours or clamp the tambours to the backing. You may force adhesive between the tambours and glue the edges together.**

QUICK FIXTURE ■ *Tambour Assembly Jig*

To properly glue up a tambour door, you need a flat surface on which to assemble the tambours. Start with a sheet of plywood a little larger than the door you want to make. Cut three wood strips from stock planed to the same thickness as the tambours. Fasten two of these near the front and back edges of the backing board. Place the third one on the board between the first two, but don't fasten it in place. Make two thicker strips and cut rabbets along their length, each rabbet as deep as the tambours are thick. Fasten these strips to the sides of the sheet. Finally, cut four or more wedges with a slope of not more than 15 degrees.

To load the tambours, remove the strip at the front of the backing sheet and slide the tambours in place between the side strips. Replace the board, fasten it down, and insert the wedges between the bottom strip and the floating strip. Arrange the wedges in pairs and tap them together to secure the tambours.

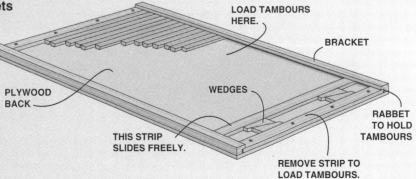

LOAD TAMBOURS HERE.

BRACKET

PLYWOOD BACK

WEDGES

THIS STRIP SLIDES FREELY.

RABBET TO HOLD TAMBOURS

REMOVE STRIP TO LOAD TAMBOURS.

ASSEMBLING THE CASE Join the sides and the back with glue, then add the trim on the outside face of the back. Before the glue dries, make sure the sides are square to the back and parallel to each other. Glue the spacer to the top, then attach the top to the case with dowels or biscuits.

Rest the completed case on its back on your workbench and feed the tambour door into its grooves. Turn the case right side up and test the sliding action of the door.

MAKING THE PIGEONHOLES To simplify the construction of the rolltop, Jim made the pigeonholes as a separate shelving unit. This unit is inserted in the case after it's assembled. Before you begin work on it, however, carefully measure the inside dimensions of the completed case. If these have changed from your plans — and they probably will have — adjust the dimensions of the pigeonhole assembly to compensate.

Also, remember that the pigeonhole design shown in the *Pigeonhole Frame Detail* is just a suggestion. You can arrange compartments of any size in any configuration you want.

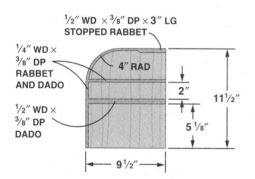

PIGEONHOLE SIDE LAYOUT

SHOP SAVVY

It will require a lot of careful, painstaking figuring to lay out the matching dowel holes on the side assembly and the top. Or, you can skip the brainwork and use dowel centers. Simply drill holes in the top surfaces of the side assembly where you want to insert dowels. Place a dowel center in each hole. Position the top over the dowel centers and press down firmly. The points on the dowel centers will leave marks on the underside of the top, showing you where to drill the matching holes.

Cut the parts to size and round the back corner of the sides and dividers, as shown in the *Pigeonhole Side Layout*. **Note: The top back corner of the side is rounded to a 4-inch radius, the dividers to 3¾ inches.**

Rout or cut the various rabbets and dadoes needed to assemble the sides, shelves, and dividers. Most of these can be cut on a table saw with a dado cutter, or with a router and a straight bit. To make the rabbets in the back edges of the pigeonhole sides, you must use a *piloted* rabbeting bit. Keep the pilot bearing on the bit against the edge of the work, in the same manner that you routed the grooves for the tambour. Also cut a stopped groove in the side or divider where you want to mount a door latch or lock.

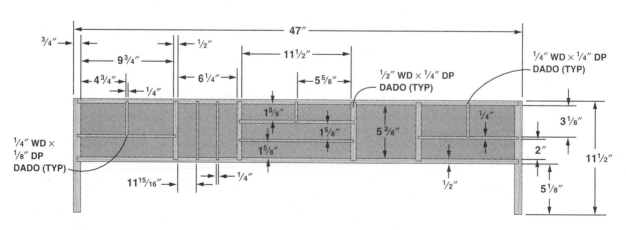

PIGEONHOLE FRAME DETAIL

Mask off the areas of the pigeonholes that will be glued together (dadoes, ends of shelves, and so on), then finish the pigeonhole parts. It's very difficult to get finish inside the small compartments *after* they're assembled.

Assemble the sides, shelves, and dividers with glue and let the glue dry completely. While you're waiting, saw ⅛-inch-deep kerfs, ¼ inch apart in the pigeonhole back where you want to bend it over the sides and dividers. Test fit it to be sure it will make the bend without breaking, then attach it with glue and brads.

MAKING THE PIGEONHOLE DRAWERS Measure the drawer openings in the completed pigeonholes and adjust the dimensions of the drawers as necessary. Cut the drawer parts, rounding off the back corner of the small drawer sides, as shown in the *Small Drawer/Side View.*

Because these are small drawers that will hold only small, light items, they don't require the sturdy joinery you used on the large pedestal drawers. Jim joined the sides to the fronts with lock joints, and the back to the sides with tongue-and-dado joints, as shown in the *Drawer Joinery Detail.* He cut grooves in the inside faces of the drawer fronts, backs, and sides to hold the drawer bottoms.

These are lipped drawers — the fronts are rabbeted around the perimeter to create a lip that partially covers the pigeonhole assembly when the drawer is closed. Additionally, Jim rabbeted the fronts of the drawer to give them the appearance of

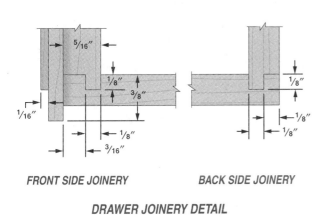

FRONT SIDE JOINERY   BACK SIDE JOINERY

DRAWER JOINERY DETAIL

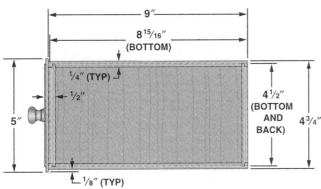

TOP VIEW

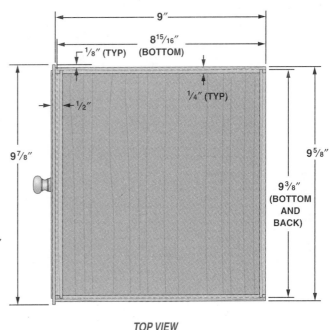

TOP VIEW

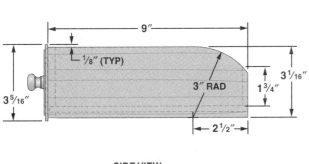

SIDE VIEW
SMALL DRAWER

SIDE VIEW
LARGE DRAWER

small raised panels. Make the joinery and decorative cuts in each drawer front in this order:

■ Cut ³⁄₁₆-inch-wide, ³⁄₈-inch-deep grooves in the ends of the drawer fronts.

■ Trim the interior side of these grooves to create tenons just ⅛ inch long.

■ Make ⁵⁄₁₆-inch-wide, ⅛-inch-deep rabbets in the top and bottom edges.

■ Cut ¼-inch-wide, ¹⁄₁₆-inch-deep rabbets in the front faces, all around the perimeter.

■ Cut a ¼-inch-wide, ¼-inch-deep groove near the bottom edge.

Also cut ⅛-inch-wide dadoes near the front ends of the sides to accept the short tenons on the drawer fronts. Cut ¼-inch-wide, ¼-inch-deep grooves in the fronts, backs, and sides for the drawer bottoms. Glue the fronts, backs, and sides together. Slide the bottoms into their grooves and secure them to the backs with brads. Don't glue them in place; let them "float."

METHODS OF WORK ■ *Making Lock Joints*

Lock joints are useful in joining the front corners of small and medium-sized drawers. They are not as rugged as dovetail joints, but they are more than adequate for drawers that will see mostly light duty.

1 **To make a lock joint,** first cut grooves in the ends of the drawer fronts. Use a tenoning jig to help hold the drawer front vertical as you make these cuts.

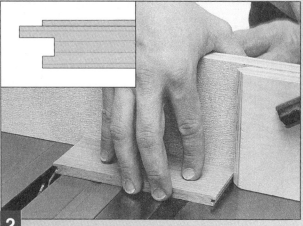

2 **When you cut the grooves,** you'll create two tongues on each end of the drawer front. Cut the inside tongues short.

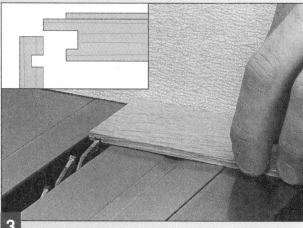

3 **Cut dadoes near the front ends** of the drawer sides. These must be as wide and as deep as the short tongues are thick and long.

HANGING THE PIGEONHOLE DOOR Like the drawer fronts, any doors you hang on the pigeonholes should be lipped. Cut ⅛-inch-wide, 5⁄16-inch-deep rabbets in the back surface of each door to make the lips, and ¼-inch-wide, 1⁄16-inch-deep rabbets in the front surface to make the decorative raised panel.

Don't cut a lip on the edge on which the door is hinged. Instead, cut mortises for butt hinges.

Drill a hole in the door for the key that turns the cupboard lock and attach the lock to the back face of the door. Attach the hinges to the door, then attach the door to the pigeonhole assembly, as shown in the *Hinge Detail*. Check that the bolt in the lock engages the slot you cut in the side or divider.

FINISHING Remove any hardware you've installed, and remove the tambours from the rolltop case. Break down the project into as many subassemblies as possible. The smaller the parts, the easier it will be to finish. Sand all the surfaces that still need it, then apply a finish. Jim used a "golden oak" aniline dye to darken the wood, then sealed this with a wash coat of shellac. (A "wash coat" is shellac that has been thinned 1 to 1 with denatured alcohol.) On top of this, he applied several coats of tung oil.

INSTALLING THE ROLLTOP Rub the inside surfaces of the tambour grooves with paraffin wax — this lubricates the tambours and helps them to slide easily. Insert the tambours in the grooves and

ALTERNATIVES

Just for a hoot, would you like to add a secret compartment to your rolltop desk? Here's a simple trick. Make one of the pigeonhole drawers short and build a smaller drawer that will slide in behind it. Attach a ribbon to the front edge of the secret drawer so you can pull it out.

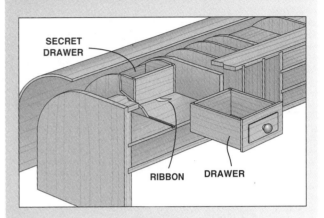

SECRET DRAWER

RIBBON   DRAWER

position the rolltop case on the desktop. Secure it by driving flathead wood screws up through the desktop and into the sides and back of the case. (You need to loosen the desktop from its pedestals to do this.)

Finally, slide the pigeonhole assembly into place in the case. Secure it by driving a flathead wood screw through each pigeonhole side and into the adjoining case side.

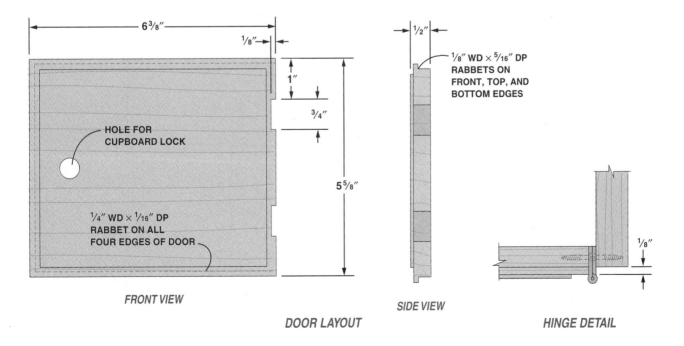

6⅜″   ⅛″

1″

¾″

HOLE FOR CUPBOARD LOCK

5⅝″

¼″ WD × 1⁄16″ DP RABBET ON ALL FOUR EDGES OF DOOR

FRONT VIEW

½″

⅛″ WD × 5⁄16″ DP RABBETS ON FRONT, TOP, AND BOTTOM EDGES

⅛″

SIDE VIEW

DOOR LAYOUT   ***HINGE DETAIL***

Portable Desk

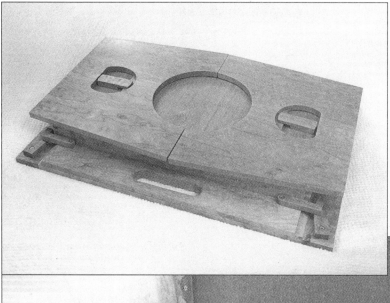

In this chapter...

PRACTICAL KNOW-HOW
Joining Breadboard Ends   89

JIGS AND FIXTURES
Finger Joint Jig   92

SHOP SOLUTIONS
Making Finger Joints   93

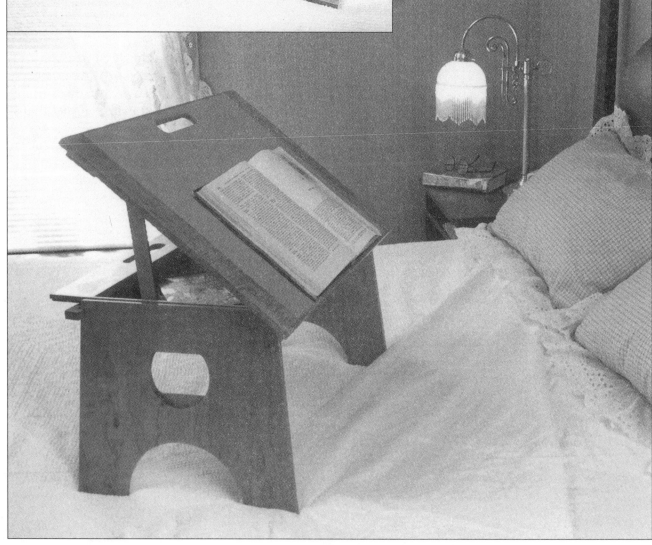

Sometimes it's nice to get away from your den or office to do some paperwork. My wife likes to pay bills while watching television; I take my laptop computer and head for the woods when a deadline is closing in. A *portable desk* helps facilitate these escapes.

The desk shown has an adequate surface on which to write checks and letters, set up a laptop computer, read a book, or make a drawing. A shallow box beneath the desk stores papers, pencils, computer diskettes, or other small items. The legs hold the desk off your legs when you use it in bed or on a couch, or they fold up out of the way when you want to rest the desk on your lap or another surface. The top tilts up to 45 degrees for the best working angle for whatever task you need to do.

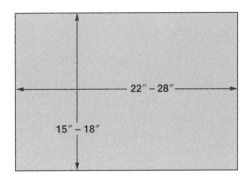

WORK SURFACE SIZE

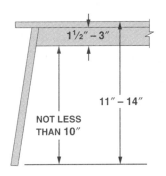

DESK HEIGHT

What size should it be?

Because this is a movable piece of furniture, the desk should be small enough and light enough to carry easily. Just as important, you want to be able to balance it on your lap. If it's too large, it may tend to tip. And if it's too heavy, it will become uncomfortable.

OVERALL SIZE AND WEIGHT A good rule of thumb is to make a portable desk about the same size and weight as a briefcase — 22 to 28 inches side to side, 15 to 18 inches front to back, and weighing no more than 7 pounds.

OTHER SIZES Three more dimensions concern you when designing a portable desk.

■ When the legs are extended, how high should the work surface be? Working at a desk, folks are most comfortable when their arms don't bend at the elbows much past 90 degrees. For this reason, the desk shouldn't be higher than 11 to 14 inches.

■ How high should you make the space beneath the desk — the kneehole or, in this case, the "lap hole"? No less than 10 inches to accommodate adult-size legs.

■ If the desk includes a storage box, how deep should it be? As shallow as possible — when the desk is resting on your lap with the legs folded, the work surface should be as close to your lap as possible. However, create enough room in the box so it's a useful storage compartment.

A portable desk shouldn't be much larger than a briefcase. In fact, for many businessmen, a briefcase makes a good portable desk.

What style will it be?

When making a portable desk, style takes a back seat to usefulness. The function of the desk dictates its form, for the most part. The portable desk shown on page 84 is designed for general purposes — it serves not only as a writing desk but also as a computer station, a drawing board, and a book stand. Desks designed for specific tasks look much different, as shown on these two pages.

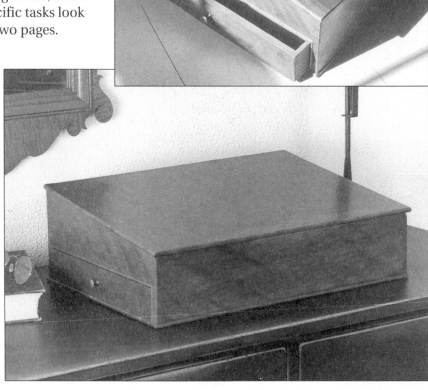

LAP DESK

The traditional form for a portable desk is the lap desk — just a small box to hold writing materials and perhaps a ledger. For hundreds of years, this was all the desk that most people needed. The lap desk shown is a copy of one made at the New Lebanon Shaker Community in New York during the first half of the nineteenth century.

PORTABLE DESK

A portable drawing board can be very useful, particularly if you need to make sketches on site. This is a drawing board that I use from time to time, in the shop or on the road. It's just a single board with fold-out feet to hold it at a slight angle when it rests on a table or a workbench. I've outfitted this board with a mechanical straightedge to help draw parallel lines, but a T-square works just as well.

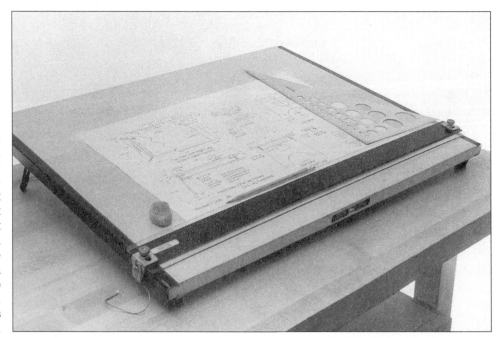

BREAKFAST TRAY

A tray with legs makes a fine desk, provided it's large enough to provide an adequate work space. The legs on this particular tray fold up so you can use it on your lap, if you so wish.

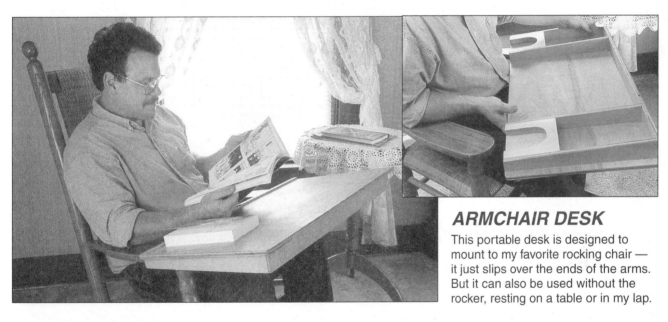

ARMCHAIR DESK

This portable desk is designed to mount to my favorite rocking chair — it just slips over the ends of the arms. But it can also be used without the rocker, resting on a table or in my lap.

LAPTOP COMPUTER DESK

This tiny S-shaped desk holds a laptop computer and hooks over your knees. It can be used sitting or reclining, as shown. This is my simplest and most successful attempt to date to design a desk that allows me to write while lying down. Unfortunately, I have yet to design something that keeps me awake while I'm using it.

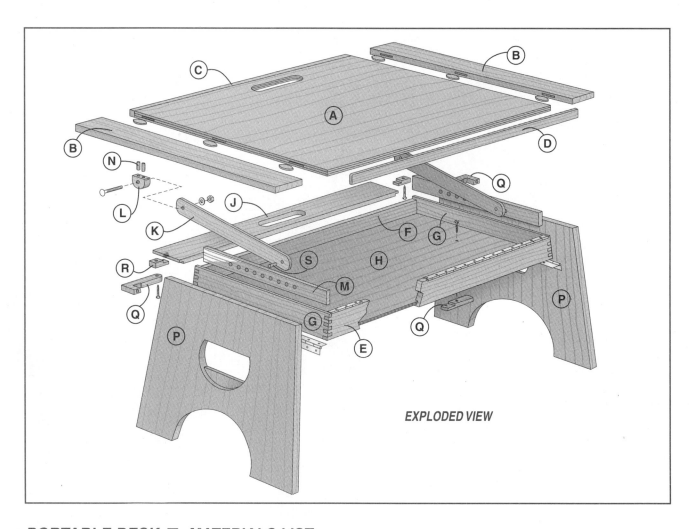

EXPLODED VIEW

PORTABLE DESK ■ MATERIALS LIST *(Finished Dimensions)*

PARTS

A	Desk top*	½″ × 15¾″ × 20″
B	Breadboard ends (2)	½″ × 2″ × 16″
C	Top edge trim	¼″ × ½″ × 20″
D	Lip	¼″ × ¾″ × 20″
E	Front	½″ × 2″ × 20″
F	Back	½″ ×1½″ × 20″
G	Sides (2)	½″ × 2″ × 12½″
H	Bottom*	¼″ × 12″ × 19½″
J	Handle	½″ × 3″ × 19″
K	Braces* (2)	¼″ × 1″ × 10″
L	Pivots* (2)	½″ × 1″ × 1″
M	Stop bar* (2)	½″ × 1″ × 11½″
N	Pivot dowels (4)	¼″ dia. × ¾″
P	Legs (2)	½″ × 12″ × 14½″
Q	Fold/extend latches (4)	½″ × 1″ × 3″

R	Top latch (2)	½″ × 1″ × 2″
S	Brace dowels (2)	¼″ dia. × ½″

*Make these parts from plywood.

HARDWARE

½″ × 20″ Piano hinge and mounting screws
½″ × 12″ Piano hinge and mounting screws (2)
³⁄₁₆″ × 1″ Carriage bolts (2)
#10 Flat washers (2)
#10 Stop nuts (2)
#8 × ¾″ Flathead wood screws (4)
#8 × ½″ Flathead wood screws (2)
#4 × ⅜″ Flathead wood screws (48)
#0 Biscuits (6)

How do I build it?

This portable desk is nothing more than a box with a few attachments. The attachments consist of a desk top, which also serves as a lid for the box, two legs to hold the desk at a comfortable working height, and latches to keep the lid closed and the legs folded.

PREPARING THE STOCK

The portable desk is made from both hardwood and plywood. Jim selected plywood for the desktop because it would help the work surface remain flat. The box bottom, braces, pivots, and stop are also plywood, while the remaining parts are made from hardwood. Start by planing the lumber to ½ inch thick. Cut the parts to size, but make the legs a little longer than specified. This gives you the extra stock necessary to bevel the top and bottom later on.

Attach the breadboard ends and top edge trim to the desktop, but hold off attaching the lip. After the glue dried on the breadboards and top trim, Jim carefully scraped the hardwood parts flush, being careful not to cut through the plywood veneer. Then he attached the lip.

METHODS OF WORK ■ Joining Breadboard Ends

To prevent wide boards such as desk and table tops from cupping, craftsmen sometimes attach "breadboards" to the ends. The wood grain in the breadboards runs perpendicular to the grain in the wider board and keeps it flat.

Unfortunately, this creates another problem. Because the wood grains are perpendicular, the breadboards restrict the normal expansion and contraction of the wide board. This often causes it to split or pop a joint. There are, however, ways to prevent this.

1 **In traditional breadboard joinery,** the breadboard is joined to the larger board with mortise-and-tenon joints. The ends of the wide board are cut with tenons to fit mortises in the breadboards. This restricts the movement of the wide board, and the resulting stress may break a tenon or split the wide board.

2 **One way to deal with** this problem is to reduce the wood movement, as we have done in the Portable Desk. Substitute a piece of plywood for the wide board. Although plywood does move slightly, the expansion and contraction will be negligible. Use splines, dowels, or biscuits to attach the breadboards to the plywood.

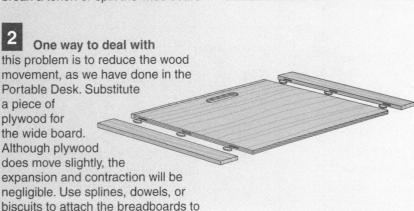

3 **If you can't use plywood,** create a joint that allows movement. Cut mortises and slots in the breadboards, then attach them to the wide board by driving roundhead screws through the slots. Plug the mortise to make the joint appear to be a mortise and tenon. As the wide board moves, the screws will slide back and forth in their slots.

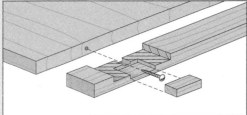

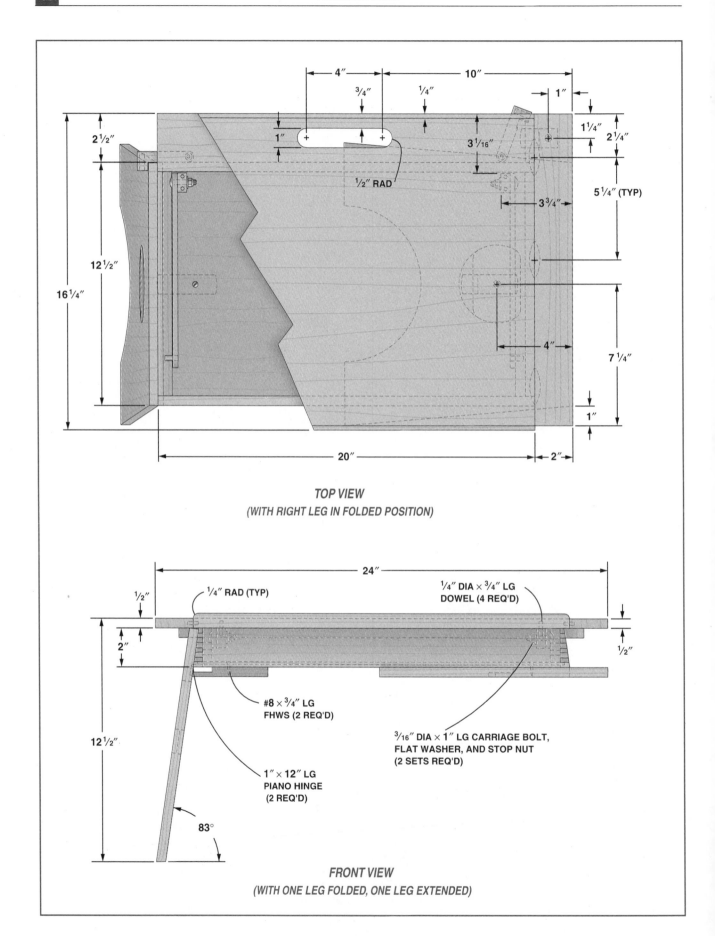

4″

10″

³⁄₄″

¼″

1″

2½″

1″

1¼″

2¼″

3¹⁄₁₆″

½″ RAD

5¼″ (TYP)

12½″

3³⁄₄″

16¼″

4″

7¼″

1″

20″

2″

TOP VIEW
(WITH RIGHT LEG IN FOLDED POSITION)

24″

¼″ RAD (TYP)

¼″ DIA × ³⁄₄″ LG
DOWEL (4 REQ'D)

½″

2″

½″

#8 × ³⁄₄″ LG
FHWS (2 REQ'D)

³⁄₁₆″ DIA × 1″ LG CARRIAGE BOLT,
FLAT WASHER, AND STOP NUT
(2 SETS REQ'D)

12½″

1″ × 12″ LG
PIANO HINGE
(2 REQ'D)

83°

FRONT VIEW
(WITH ONE LEG FOLDED, ONE LEG EXTENDED)

MAKING THE JOINERY

Because so many of the parts on this project move, there is little joinery. Most parts are attached with hinges, bolts, or screws.

DRILLING THE HOLES The braces hold the desk top at different angles, up to 45 degrees from horizontal. One end of the brace swings on a pivot block, while the other holds a short dowel that locks into position in holes in the stop bar. Drill ³⁄₁₆-inch-diameter holes in the pivot block and braces for the pivot bolts, and ¼-inch-diameter holes in the braces and stop bars for the dowels. Also drill ¼-inch-diameter holes in the top surfaces of the pivot blocks. Later, you'll use these holes to attach the blocks to the underside of the desk top with dowels.

MAKING A FEW RABBETS Cut rabbets and notches in the ends of the handle. The notches fit

around the sides when the box is assembled. The top latches fit over the rabbets in the handle, holding the box closed.

MAKING THE BOX JOINERY The front, back, and sides of the box are joined with finger joints. This is an especially strong joint, and it helps keep the shallow box flat. It's useful not only for this project but also for other desk projects that require small drawers. "Pigeonhole" drawers are often assembled with finger joints for strength and durability. Jim and I also like the way they look, which was the real reason we chose them. You can also use dovetails, splined miters, interlocking rabbets, or other corner joints.

After cutting the finger joints, rout ⅛-inch-wide grooves in the inside faces of the front, back, and sides to hold the bottom. These grooves are stopped at each end; they don't extend to the ends of the boards. If they did, you would see them when you assemble the box.

Cut rabbets around the four edges of the bottom so the bottom will fit the grooves. When assembled, the outside face of the bottom should be flush with the lower edges of the box.

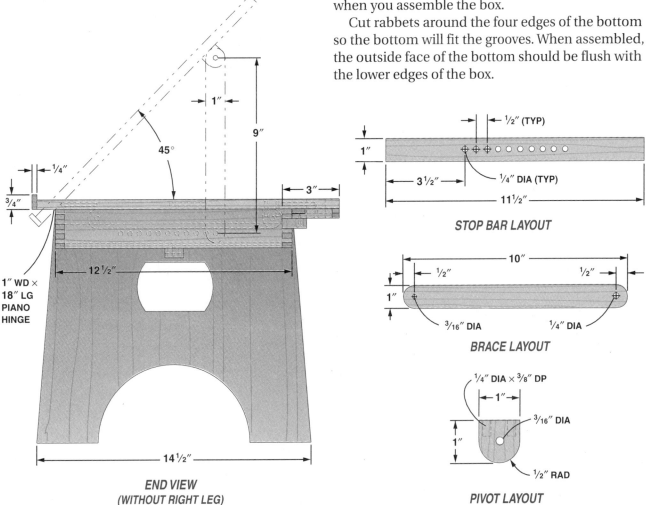

END VIEW
(WITHOUT RIGHT LEG)

STOP BAR LAYOUT

BRACE LAYOUT

PIVOT LAYOUT

QUICK FIXTURE ■ *Finger Joint Jig*

The finger joint jig is an adjustable miter gauge extension. One part — the fixed face — mounts to the miter gauge. The other — the sliding face — moves from side to side. A machine screw set in an adjustment block enables you to adjust the position of the sliding extension in minute increments.

Before you make the fixture, decide the width of the fingers you wish to cut. This determines the width of the stop in the sliding face. If you plan to use this fixture to cut fingers of different sizes, make several sliding faces, each with a different size stop.

Drill counterbored holes for carriage bolts in the sliding face, and cut corresponding slots in the fixed face. This lets you move the sliding face from side to side, then lock it in place with the carriage bolts.

Drill and countersink a 5/32-inch-diameter hole through the adjustment block and thread a #10-32 machine screw in the hole. The fit will be a little snug, but that's exactly what you want. When you turn the machine screw, it will hold its position.

The reason for using a #10-32 machine screw is that it has precisely 32 threads per linear inch. One complete turn of the screw moves it horizontally 1/32 inch. One half turn moves it 1/64 inch; one-quarter turn, 1/128 inch. This lets you make exacting adjustments. Thread a knurled knob onto the end of the screw and hold it in place with a stop nut. This will allow you to turn the screw without reaching for a screwdriver.

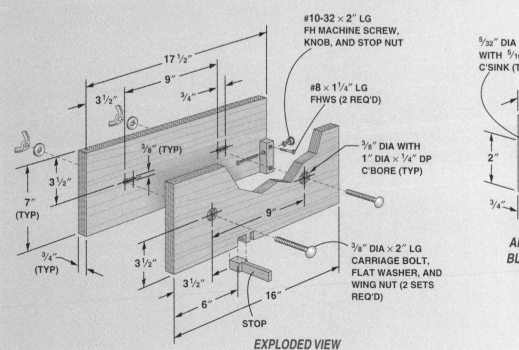

#10-32 × 2″ LG
FH MACHINE SCREW,
KNOB, AND STOP NUT

17 1/2″

9″

3 1/2″

3/4″

#8 × 1 1/4″ LG
FHWS (2 REQ'D)

3/8″ (TYP)

3/8″ DIA WITH
1″ DIA × 1/4″ DP
C'BORE (TYP)

3 1/2″

7″
(TYP)

9″

3/4″
(TYP)

3 1/2″

3/8″ DIA × 2″ LG
CARRIAGE BOLT,
FLAT WASHER, AND
WING NUT (2 SETS
REQ'D)

3 1/2″

6″

16″

STOP

EXPLODED VIEW

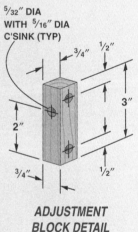

5/32″ DIA
WITH 5/16″ DIA
C'SINK (TYP)

3/4″   1/2″

3″

2″

3/4″   1/2″

*ADJUSTMENT
BLOCK DETAIL*

METHODS OF WORK ■ *Making Finger Joints*

A finger joint joins two boards with interlocking tenons and notches. In most cases, the fingers and notches are spaced evenly, and they are all the same dimensions.

When making a finger joint, rip the adjoining boards to a width that is a multiple of the finger width. There should be no split fingers in the joint. Cut the fingers $\frac{1}{32}$ to $\frac{1}{16}$ inch longer than needed so the fingers protrude slightly when you assemble the joint. (After assembly, sand the fingers flush.) To prevent tear-out and chipping, back up the boards with a scrap as you make the fingers.

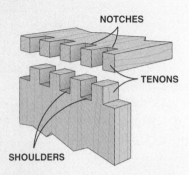

NOTCHES

TENONS

SHOULDERS

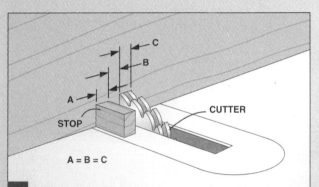

C

B

A

STOP

CUTTER

A = B = C

1 **You can cut a finger joint** on a table saw outfitted with a dado cutter or a router table and a straight bit — the procedure is the same. I prefer the table saw; the rotation of a router bit tends to pull your work sideways. Attach an auxiliary extension with a stop to the miter gauge. The stop must be the same width as the dado cutter or router bit. Adjust the extension so the distance between the stop and the cutter is the same as the cutter and the stop (A=B=C).

2 **Place the first board** on end against the miter gauge extension and butt one edge against the stop. Clamp the board to the extension to prevent it from shifting, then feed the board into the cutter with the miter gauge, cutting the first notch.

3 **Place the second board** against the first, face to face, aligning the edge of the second board with the side of the notch nearest the stop. Clamp the second board to the first and cut a notch in the corner of the second board.

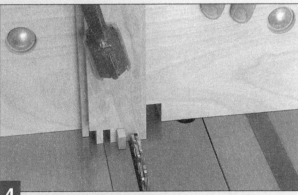

4 **Loosen the clamps** and move both boards sideways, fitting the notches over the stop. Secure the boards to the extension again and cut a second set of notches. Repeat until you have cut all the notches in both boards. **Note: If the joint is too tight, move the stop *toward* the cutter slightly. If it's too loose, move it *away* from the cutter.**

MAKING THE LEGS

Cut the legs from hardwood boards, tapering them slightly and beveling the top and bottom edges at 7 degrees. Cut a half circle in the bottom of each leg for the feet, then rout the cut-outs.

MAKING THE CUTOUTS One edge of each cutout is rabbeted, as shown in the *Leg Detail*. Latches engage the rabbeted edges to keep the legs folded or press against the surface of the legs to help keep them extended.

Create the cutouts with a little pattern routing. To do this, you need a template. Using a hole saw, cut a 4-inch-diameter circle in a scrap of stock. (This stock must be as thick as the router bit's cutting flutes are long.) Keep the plug and cut two ¾-inch-wide flat-sided "inserts" for the template, as shown in the photos below. Secure the inserts to

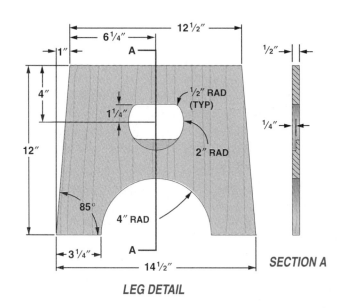

LEG DETAIL

SECTION A

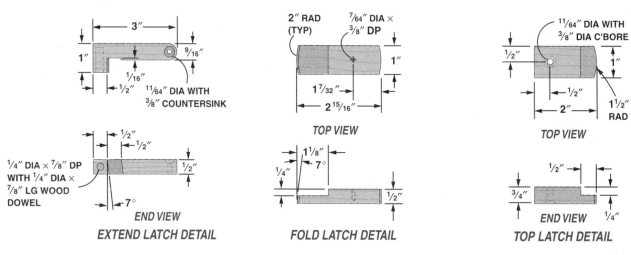

EXTEND LATCH DETAIL

FOLD LATCH DETAIL

TOP LATCH DETAIL

Create a template for a circular cutout and secure inserts inside the cutout so the circle has two flat sides, top and bottom. Attach the template to a leg. Using a pattern-routing bit (a straight bit with a guide bearing), rout completely through the stock.

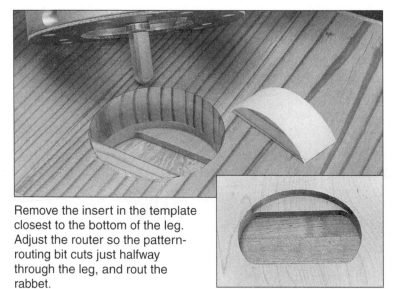

Remove the insert in the template closest to the bottom of the leg. Adjust the router so the pattern-routing bit cuts just halfway through the leg, and rout the rabbet.

the inside edges of the template with double-faced carpet tape, making a circle with two flat sides, top and bottom.

Secure the template to the leg and rout completely through it. Then remove one insert from the template and rout partway through the stock, creating a rabbet on the flat side of the cutout nearest the bottom edge of the leg. Repeat for the second leg.

Also make the cutouts in the top and the handle. Secure the handle to the top with carpet tape and drill two holes through the parts to mark the ends of the cutouts. Remove the waste between the holes and round over the edges.

ASSEMBLING THE DESK

Finish sand the parts that you've made and assemble the front, back, sides, and handle with glue. As you put the box parts together, slide the bottom in place in the assembly. However, don't glue it. Instead, let it float in the grooves.

After the glue dries, sand the assembled finger joints flush and bevel the sides. Attach the pivot blocks to the top with dowels and glue, and cut the hinge mortises in the box parts.

FINISHING THE PARTS It's best to finish the box and the other parts of the portable desk before final assembly. Do any necessary touch-up sanding on the wooden surfaces, then apply a finish. Jim used a wipe-on tung oil finish for this project.

FINAL ASSEMBLY Attach the legs to the sides and the desk top to the front with piano hinges. When folded, the bottoms of the legs should just touch one another. Install the latches that keep the top closed, the legs folded, and the legs extended. To extend the legs, turn the "fold" latches parallel to the sides. Raise the legs, then pivot the "extend" latches to lock the legs in place.

SHOP SAVVY

Pivots tend to work themselves loose as the parts turn. There are ways to prevent this, however. When using a bolt for a pivot, secure it with a *stop nut*. These have plastic inserts on the insides to keep the nuts from turning. When using a screw as a pivot, put a drop of epoxy in the pilot hole. Drive the screw into the hole before the epoxy hardens.

To make the handle cutout, clamp the handle to the desktop. Drill holes where you want the ends of the cutout, then remove the waste between the holes with a saber saw or scroll saw.

When extended, the legs should be slightly splayed — this makes the desk more stable. To create this splay, bevel the sides of the assembled box at 7 degrees. Do this on a table saw, using a miter gauge extension with a stop to help feed the box over the blade.

The "extend" leg latches not only capture the legs but they also brace the legs when they are extended.

Computer Secretary

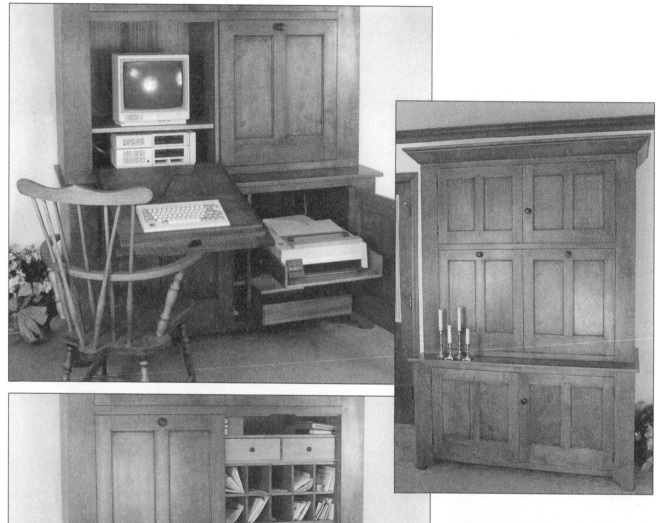

In this chapter...

PRACTICAL KNOW-HOW

| Sizing a Secretary | 97 |
| Making a Writing Surface | 113 |

JIGS AND FIXTURES

| Miter Shooting Block | 111 |
| Tenoning Jig | 111 |

SHOP SOLUTIONS

| Joining Door Frames with Decorative Edges | 110 |
| Driving Square Pegs in Round Holes | 112 |

David T. Smith, a master craftsman and accomplished furniture maker, renowned for his Country-style furniture, was dealing with a difficult request when he designed this Country Secretary desk. His client wanted both a writing desk and a computer desk in the same piece of furniture — she didn't have room for both. Additionally, she didn't want a computer desk that looked like a computer desk. In fact, she wanted to be able to hide the computer completely so as not to clash with her classic and country decor.

David's solution was to hide both desks in a huge chest-on-chest — two cabinets stacked vertically. When the right top case and the bottom left case were open, the piece would function as a secretary and a filing cabinet. When the left top case and the bottom right case were open, it would be a computer desk and printer stand. And when both cases were closed, it would appear as a large clothes press or *armoire*.

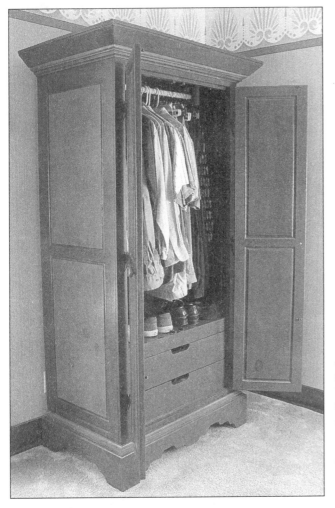

What size should it be?

Clothes presses, linen cupboards, wardrobes, and armoires all belong to a family of large cabinets that were popular for centuries before the turn of the century. During that time, houses were commonly built without closets. These large pieces provided the storage space needed for clothes and linens. Because some clothes needed to be hung and others folded, they were usually quite tall, some well over 7 feet in height. They were wide as well, often 4 feet or more. Some, in fact, were so massive, that they came apart into flat panels — front, sides, back, and so on — just so they could be moved.

Since the turn of the twentieth century, these pieces have been adapted for other purposes, particularly desks and entertainment centers. David's design fits *two* desks in an armoire. Each desk is 24 inches wide. This is somewhat cramped if you need to spread out when you write or compute, but you can double the desk space by opening both drop-down work surfaces.

The desk must be tall enough to accommodate a computer monitor (15 to 17 inches), and space to store a keyboard and a mouse (2 to 3 inches) above the work surface, which is about 30 inches off the floor. Add shelving space for a few books above the monitor, and the desk becomes about 72 inches tall. Add a second book shelf, and you get to 84 inches, the height of David's desk.

The desk must be deep enough to hold a computer CPU and monitor (15 to 18 inches). David decided on a "step-back" design, making the top section 18 inches deep and the bottom section 25 inches, the same as a standard filing cabinet. However, if you don't need the file storage space, you can make the cabinet straight up and down.

A typical wardrobe or armoire offered a great deal of storage space. Typically, there were drawers in the bottom for clothes and linens that could be folded and a tall cupboard space above for hanging clothes. This arrangement can be easily adapted to hold audio and video equipment. By adding a drop-down or pull-out work surface, it can hold computer equipment as well.

What style will it be?

David T. Smith's computer secretary is built in what has come to be called a Country style. Country furniture is actually made along the same lines as *classic* furniture — the Queen Anne, Chippendale, Federal, and American Empire styles that were built before the Industrial Revolution. However, the designs are scaled back to make them simpler and less time-consuming to build. Cabinetmakers who catered to farmers and working-class folk did this because their clientele could not afford the high style.

Crafted by Jim McCann, Brookville, Ohio.

CHIPPENDALE STYLE

In 1754, Thomas Chippendale, an English designer, published *The Gentleman and Cabinet-Maker's Director,* a pattern book of ornate furniture. The elaborate style quickly caught on with high society on both sides of the Atlantic, although the American interpretation was more reserved and straightforward. The imposing pediment top (meant to suggest the roofs of Greek and Roman temples) and the ornate frame base make this an American Chippendale cabinet.

Crafted by Kendl Monn, Christiana, Pennsylvania. Photo by Jonathan Bizen.

PENNSYLVANIA GERMAN STYLE

In the early eighteenth century, German settlers banded together in tight enclaves outside of Philadelphia, where they carefully preserved their own traditions. Among these were the design traditions for their furniture. This *Kast* is a wardrobe made in the ancient German tradition.

Crafted by Michael Cabanniss, Albion, California.

SOUTHWEST STYLE

When the Spanish conquered the southwestern portion of the American continent in the sixteenth century, they found the natives already had highly developed woodworking skills. As part of their missionary efforts, the Spanish taught the natives to build European furniture. The Spanish designs were a unique blend of European and African art forms. When the African Moors ruled Spain during medieval times, the Spanish adopted their design traditions. Native American woodworkers found these similar to their own. The two decorative styles combined to create the unique Southwest style. This ventilated cabinet is a modern interpretation.

CONTEMPORARY STYLE

After the turn of the twentieth century, craftsmen began to use fewer decorative elements in their designs. "Form follows function" became the watchword. This aesthetic principle finally culminated in the Contemporary style — light, economical, and versatile forms that became popular after World War II.

Crafted by Daniel Garber, Clayton, Ohio.

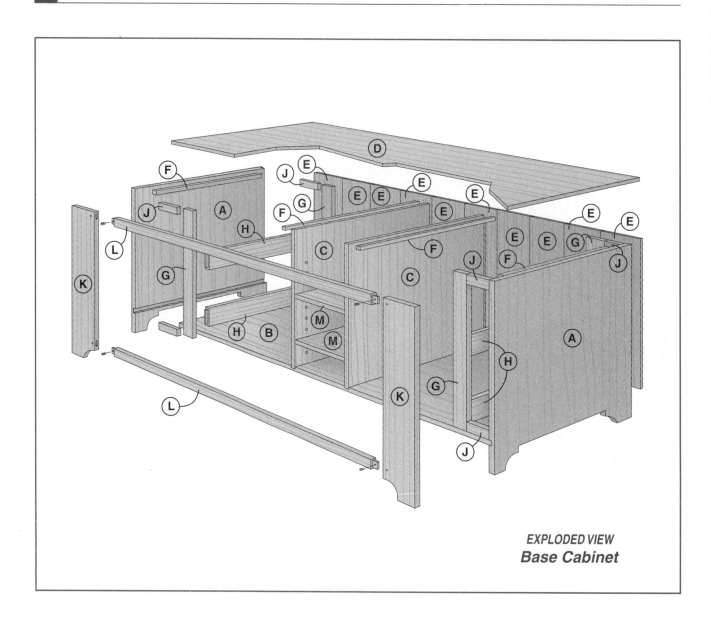

EXPLODED VIEW
Base Cabinet

COMPUTER SECRETARY ■ *MATERIALS LIST* (Finished Dimensions)

PARTS — BASE CABINET

A	Sides (2)	¾″ × 24¼″ × 29″	**L**	Face frame rails (2)	¾″ × 1½″ × 50″
B	Bottom shelf	¾″ × 23⅞″ × 57¼″	**M**	Adjustable shelves (2)	¾″ × 23⅞″ × 9⅞″
C	Dividers (2)	¾″ × 23⅞″ × 24½″			
D	Counter	¾″ × 26″ × 60″			
E	Backboards (10)	⅜″ × 6″ (approx.) × 24⅞″			
F	Cleats (4)	¾″ × ¾″ × 22⅜″		**HARDWARE**	
G	Support frame stiles (4)	¾″ × 2″ × 24⅛″		Shelving support pins (8)	
H	Support frame rails (4)	¾″ × 3½″ × 23⅛″		#8 × 1¼″ Roundhead wood screws (24)	
J	Spacers (8)	¾″ × 1½″ × 3½″		#8 × 1″ Flathead wood screws (6)	
K	Face frame stiles (2)	¾″ × 5″ × 29″		1″ Wire brads (60)	

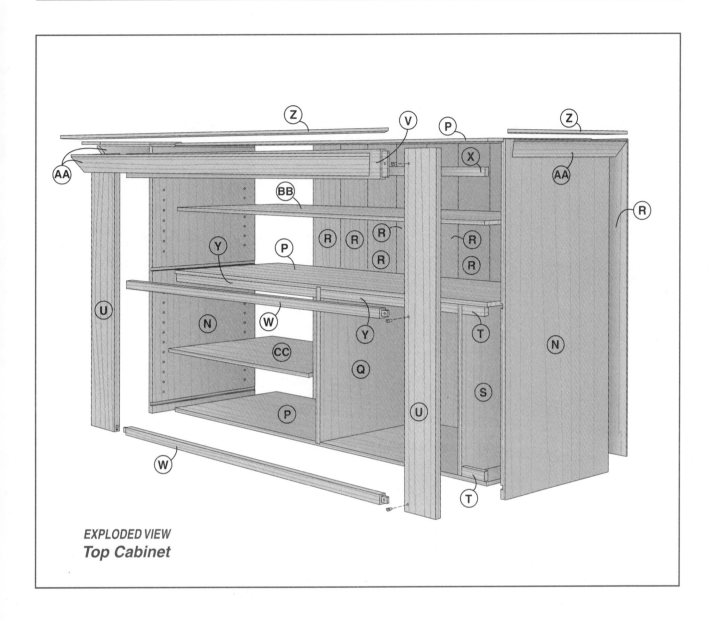

EXPLODED VIEW
Top Cabinet

COMPUTER SECRETARY ■ MATERIALS LIST *(Finished Dimensions)*

PARTS — TOP CABINET

N	Sides (2)	$\frac{3}{4}'' \times 18\frac{1}{4}'' \times 53\frac{1}{2}''$
P	Fixed shelves (3)	$\frac{3}{4}'' \times 17\frac{7}{8}'' \times 57\frac{1}{4}''$
Q	Divider	$\frac{3}{4}'' \times 17\frac{7}{8}'' \times 28''$
R	Backboards (10)	$\frac{3}{8}'' \times 6''$ (approx.) $\times 53\frac{1}{2}''$
S	False side	$\frac{3}{4}'' \times 17\frac{7}{8}'' \times 27\frac{1}{4}''$
T	Spacers (4)	$\frac{3}{4}'' \times 1\frac{1}{2}'' \times 3\frac{1}{2}''$
U	Face frame stiles (2)	$\frac{3}{4}'' \times 5'' \times 53\frac{1}{2}''$
V	Top face frame rail	$\frac{3}{4}'' \times 4\frac{1}{2}'' \times 50''$
W	Middle/bottom face frame rails (2)	$\frac{3}{4}'' \times 1\frac{1}{2}'' \times 50''$
X	Top door stop	$\frac{3}{4}'' \times 1\frac{1}{2}'' \times 56\frac{1}{2}''$

Y	Bottom door stops (2)	$\frac{3}{4}'' \times 1\frac{1}{2}'' \times 23\frac{5}{8}''$
Z	Soffit (total)	$\frac{3}{4}'' \times 5'' \times 124''$
AA	Sprung molding (total)	$\frac{3}{4}'' \times 4\frac{1}{4}'' \times 124''$
BB	Long adjustable shelf	$1'' \times 17\frac{7}{8}'' \times 56\frac{1}{2}''$
CC	Short adjustable shelf (optional)	$1'' \times 17\frac{7}{8}'' \times 28\frac{1}{4}''$

HARDWARE

Shelving support pins (4–8)

#8 × 1¼″ Flathead wood screws (33)

1″ Wire brads (66)

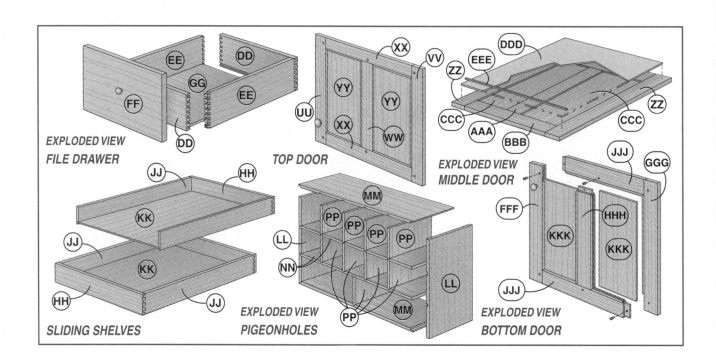

EXPLODED VIEW
FILE DRAWER

TOP DOOR

EXPLODED VIEW
MIDDLE DOOR

SLIDING SHELVES

EXPLODED VIEW
PIGEONHOLES

EXPLODED VIEW
BOTTOM DOOR

PARTS — FILE DRAWERS

DD	Fronts/backs (4)	$\frac{3}{4}'' \times 6'' \times 14''$
EE	Sides (4)	$\frac{1}{2}'' \times 6'' \times 22\frac{3}{4}''$
FF	Faces (2)	$\frac{3}{4}'' \times 11\frac{1}{4}'' \times 15''$
GG	Bottoms (2)	$\frac{1}{4}'' \times 13\frac{1}{4}'' \times 22\frac{1}{2}''$

PARTS — SLIDING SHELVES

HH	Fronts/backs (3–4)	$\frac{3}{4}'' \times 3\frac{1}{2}'' \times 18''$
JJ	Sides (4)	$\frac{1}{2}'' \times 3\frac{1}{2}'' \times 22\frac{3}{4}''$
KK	Bottoms (2)	$\frac{1}{4}'' \times 17\frac{1}{4}'' \times 22\frac{1}{2}''$

PARTS — PIGEONHOLES

LL	Sides (2)	$\frac{1}{2}'' \times 8'' \times 16\frac{1}{2}''$
MM	Top/bottom (2)	$\frac{1}{2}'' \times 8'' \times 23\frac{1}{2}''$
NN	Shelves (2)	$\frac{1}{2}'' \times 8'' \times 23''$
PP	Dividers (9)	$\frac{1}{2}'' \times 8'' \times 5\frac{1}{2}''$
QQ	Drawer fronts (2)	$\frac{3}{4}'' \times 5'' \times 11''$
RR	Drawer sides (4)	$\frac{1}{2}'' \times 5'' \times 7\frac{5}{8}''$
SS	Drawer backs (2)	$\frac{1}{2}'' \times 4\frac{1}{2}'' \times 10\frac{1}{2}''$
TT	Drawer bottoms (2)	$\frac{1}{4}'' \times 7\frac{1}{2}'' \times 10\frac{1}{2}''$

PARTS — TOP DOORS

UU	Outside stiles (2)	$\frac{3}{4}'' \times 2\frac{3}{4}'' \times 19\frac{1}{2}''$
VV	Inside stiles (2)	$\frac{3}{4}'' \times 3\frac{1}{4}'' \times 19\frac{1}{2}''$
WW	Middle stiles (2)	$\frac{3}{4}'' \times 3'' \times 16\frac{1}{2}''$
XX	Rails (4)	$\frac{3}{4}'' \times 2\frac{3}{4}'' \times 21''$

YY	Panels (2)	$\frac{1}{4}'' \times 8\frac{1}{8}'' \times 14\frac{1}{2}''$

PARTS — MIDDLE DOORS

ZZ	Outside stiles (4)	$\frac{3}{4}'' \times 2\frac{3}{4}'' \times 26\frac{1}{2}''$
AAA	Middle stiles (2)	$\frac{3}{4}'' \times 3'' \times 23\frac{1}{2}''$
BBB	Rails (4)	$\frac{3}{4}'' \times 2\frac{3}{4}'' \times 21''$
CCC	Panels (2)	$\frac{1}{4}'' \times 8\frac{1}{8}'' \times 21\frac{1}{2}''$
DDD	Work surfaces (2)	$\frac{1}{4}'' \times 22\frac{1}{2}'' \times 25''$
EEE	Pencil ledge	$\frac{1}{4}'' \times \frac{1}{4}'' \times 22\frac{1}{2}''$

PARTS — BOTTOM DOORS

FFF	Outside stiles (2)	$\frac{3}{4}'' \times 2\frac{3}{4}'' \times 23''$
GGG	Inside stiles (4)	$\frac{3}{4}'' \times 3\frac{1}{4}'' \times 23''$
HHH	Middle stiles (2)	$\frac{3}{4}'' \times 3'' \times 20''$
JJJ	Rails (4)	$\frac{3}{4}'' \times 2\frac{3}{4}'' \times 21''$
KKK	Panels (2)	$\frac{1}{4}'' \times 8\frac{1}{8}'' \times 18''$

HARDWARE

22″ Full extension slides and mounting screws (8)

$1\frac{1}{2}'' \times 2\frac{1}{2}''$ Butt hinges and mounting screws (12)

$1\frac{1}{2}''$ Pulls (6)

Door catches (6)

#8 × 1″ Ovalhead wood screws (8)

#8 Finishing washers (8)

How do I build it?

Because the desk is a large piece, David built it in two sections — a top and a bottom case — to make it easier to move. The bottom case hides drawers and pull-out shelves on full extension slides. The top case is a shelving unit with space for computer components, books, and papers. If you have a spacious shop, you may want to build both cases at the same time. The tool setups used to make them are the same for both, and you can save some time. However, if space is limited, build one at a time.

PREPARING THE MATERIALS

David's desk is built from cherry, but you can use almost any cabinet-grade hardwood. To keep his furniture true to the historical designs that inspire him, David avoids the use of plywood. *Everything* is made from solid wood. It also opens up the variety of woods in which he can work. If he were to make a piece from both lumber and plywood, he'd have to purchase a plywood with a veneer surface that matched the solid wood. These are commonly available only in a few species.

WORKING WITH SOLID WOOD If you choose to follow David's example, you'll need to purchase about 200 board feet of hardwood. Resaw enough of this lumber to make the door panels and drawer bottoms, and plane it down to $\frac{1}{4}$ inch thick. Then choose the stock for the back boards and the pigeonholes, and plane it to $\frac{3}{8}$ inch thick. Plane the remaining stock to $\frac{3}{4}$ inch thick, and glue up the wide stock you'll need to make the sides, dividers, and shelves. Cut the case parts to size, but hold off on the others.

The back slats overlap one another. Cut interlocking rabbets, $\frac{3}{8}$-inch-wide and $\frac{3}{16}$-inch deep, in the edges of the slats, as shown in the *Back Joinery Detail*. Stain the surfaces of the rabbets a dark color, or the same color that you plan for the finished desk. Because these slats are solid wood,

they will shrink and swell with the seasons. If the rabbets are left a light color, the gaps between the boards will stick out when the wood shrinks.

WORKING WITH PLYWOOD Should you prefer to make this piece out of a mixture of solid wood and plywood, substitute $\frac{1}{4}$ inch plywood for the $\frac{1}{4}$- and $\frac{3}{8}$-inch-thick parts. Change the width of the rabbets that hold the back to $\frac{1}{4}$ inch, and increase the width of the shelves by $\frac{1}{8}$ inch.

MAKING THE CASES

Both the top and bottom case are large boxes, open at the front. The front edges of each box are covered with a face frame.

MAKING THE JOINERY The cases are assembled with a simple system of rabbets and dadoes. For the most part, these are cut in the sides:

- $\frac{3}{4}$-inch-wide, $\frac{3}{8}$-inch-deep dadoes in the top and base sides to hold the shelves, as shown in the *Top and Base Side Layout*
- $\frac{3}{4}$-inch-wide, $\frac{3}{8}$-inch-deep rabbets in the top side to hold the top shelf
- $\frac{3}{4}$-inch-wide, $\frac{3}{8}$-inch-deep dadoes in the fixed shelves to hold the dividers, as shown in the *Front View* and *Section A*
- If you're making a solid wood back, $\frac{3}{8}$-inch-wide, $\frac{3}{8}$-inch-deep rabbets in the back edges of the sides
- If you're making a plywood back, $\frac{1}{4}$-inch-wide, $\frac{3}{8}$-inch-deep rabbets in the back edges of the sides
- If you're making a solid wood back, a $\frac{3}{8}$-inch-wide, $\frac{3}{8}$-inch-deep stopped rabbet in the back edge of the counter, as shown in the *Counter Detail/Bottom View*
- If you're making a plywood back, a $\frac{1}{4}$-inch-wide, $\frac{3}{8}$-inch-deep stopped rabbet in the back edge of the counter

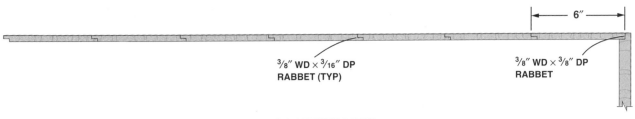

$\frac{3}{8}$" WD × $\frac{3}{16}$" DP RABBET (TYP)

$\frac{3}{8}$" WD × $\frac{3}{8}$" DP RABBET

6"

BACK JOINERY DETAIL

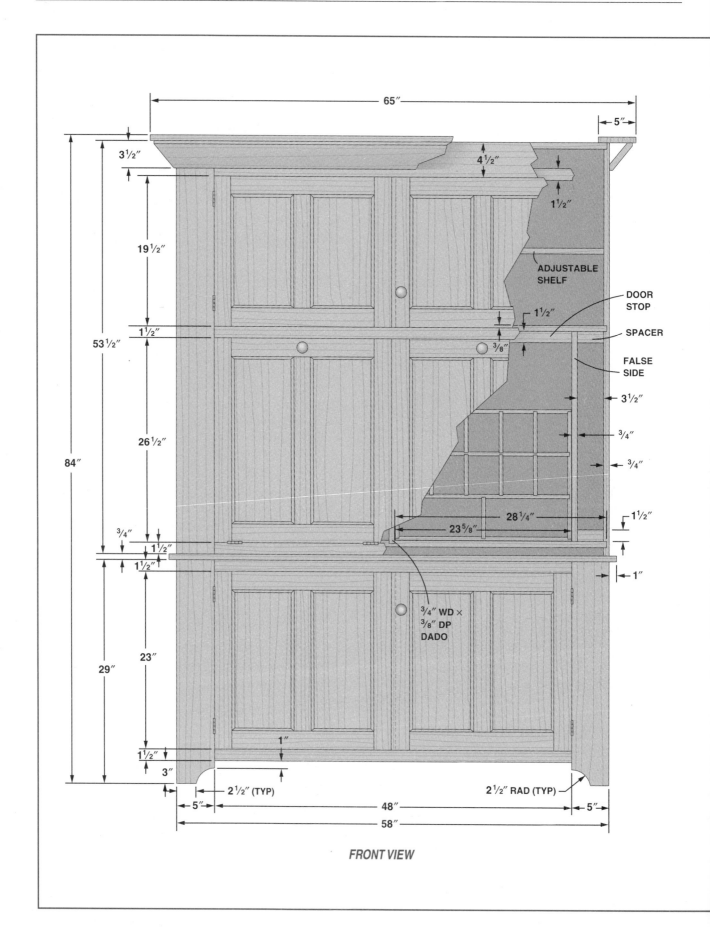

FRONT VIEW

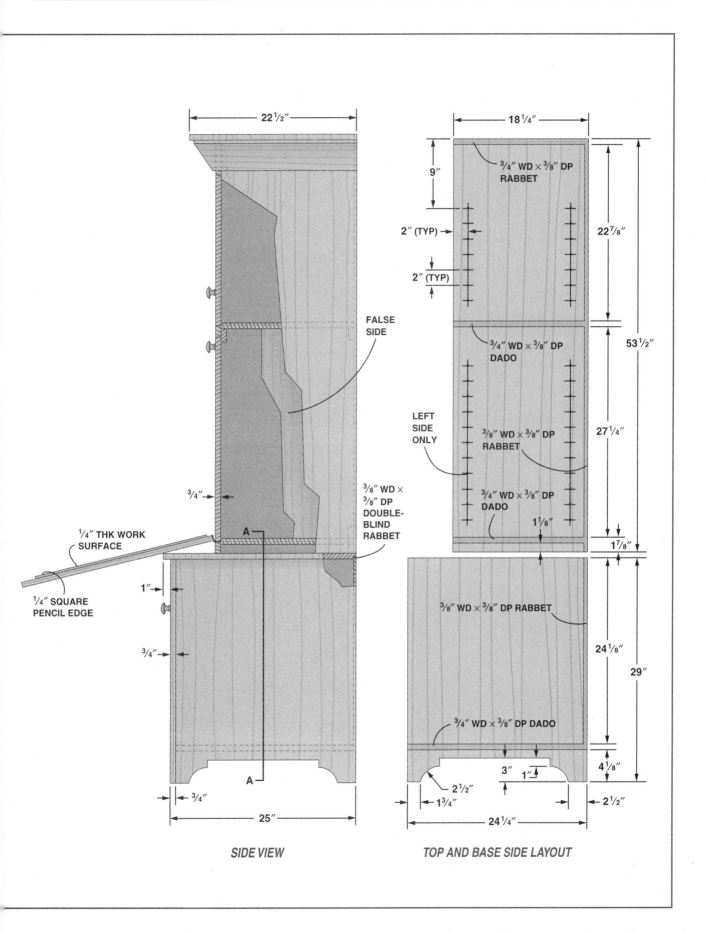

SIDE VIEW

TOP AND BASE SIDE LAYOUT

DRILLING THE SUPPORT HOLES The shelves in the top case are supported by movable pins. These pins rest in rows of holes, as shown in the *Top and Base Side Layout.* Drill the holes in the top sides and the top divider with a portable drill, using a drilling guide to position them precisely.

> **Look Here! For more information on drilling the support holes and using a drilling guide, see page 15.**

Also drill support holes in the inside faces of the two base dividers, as shown in the *Base Divider Layout.* These support the short shelves between the drawer and the sliding shelves.

MAKING THE SUPPORT FRAMES Inside the base cabinet, the drawers and sliding shelves are mounted to the dividers and to two support frames. Each frame consists of two vertical stiles and two horizontal rails. The stiles are attached to the back and to the face frame, allowing you to mount extension slides on the rails.

Cut mortises in the faces of the stiles, then matching tenons in the ends of the rails, as shown in the *Drawer Support Assembly* drawings. Note that David positioned the rails at different levels on each frame.

ALTERNATIVES

If you wish, you can substitute two biscuits for each of the mortise-and-tenon joints in the support frames. The double biscuit joints are strong enough to support the weight of the drawers.

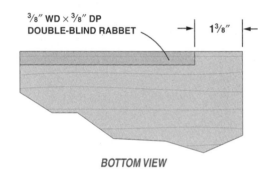

³⁄₈″ WD × ³⁄₈″ DP DOUBLE-BLIND RABBET   1³⁄₈″

BOTTOM VIEW
COUNTER DETAIL

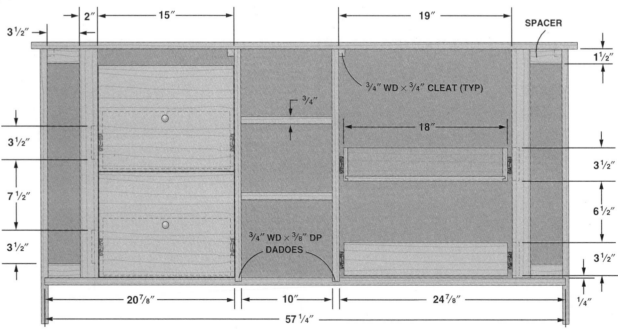

FRONT VIEW
BASE (WITHOUT FACING AND DOORS)

ASSEMBLING THE BASE CABINET At this point, I suggest that you assemble the cabinets. On another project, I might advise you to make the face frame before assembly, but that's not necessarily the wisest course of action here. You're going to be crawling in and out of the base cabinet as you put it together, and this will be easier to do without the face frame in place. Also, large cabinets have an annoying habit of changing dimensions a fraction of an inch as they're built. If you fit the frame to the case after it's assembled, you can compensate for this anomaly.

Drill oversize pilot holes in the cleats, slightly bigger than the screw shank. The holes will allow the sides, dividers, and counter to expand and contract even after the cleats are attached. Attach a cleat to each side and each divider, flush with the top edge, as shown in *Section A*.

Glue the sides and the bottom shelf together, keeping the corners at the proper angle with corners squares. Add the counter, fastening it in place by driving roundhead screws up through the side cleats. Next, install the cleats and the dividers, gluing the dividers in the dadoes in

> **Look Here! For more information on corner squares, see page 33.**

the bottom shelf and screwing the cleats to the underside of the counter. To keep the assembly square, attach the backboards (or the plywood back) to the sides, shelf, and counter with brads.

TRY THIS!

To help measure the positions of the support frame accurately, cut two slender sticks, 15 inches and 19 inches long. Use these as "feeler gauges" to gauge the distance between the rails and the dividers.

Finally attach the support frames. This is where it becomes necessary to climb in and out of the case. The rails on the support frame must be perfectly parallel to the dividers for the drawers and shelves to slide smoothly. Glue spacers to the bottom shelf and the counter to help position the frames, but also check with a measuring device that the frames are parallel.

ASSEMBLING THE TOP CABINET The procedure for assembling the top cabinet is similar. Glue the sides to the fixed shelves and attach the backboards to keep the assembly square. Glue spacers to the middle and bottom shelves, against the right side, then screw the false side to the spacers. (If you'd like a secret compartment, cut the false side in two parts, 12 inches and 6 inches wide, approximately. Hinge the narrower part with invisible Soss hinges so it opens like a door. Attach a ribbon to the front edge to serve as a pull.

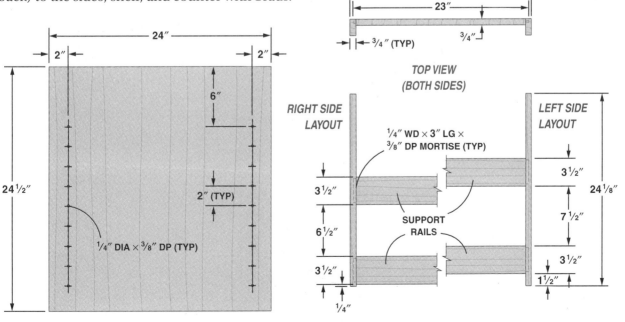

BASE DIVIDER LAYOUT

DRAWER SUPPORT ASSEMBLY

MAKING AND INSTALLING THE FACE FRAMES

Carefully measure the assembled cases and make any necessary adjustments in the sizes of the face frames. Cut the scallops in the bottom inside corners of the base stiles, as shown in the *Front View*, then join the frame members.

As shown in the *Face Frame Joinery Detail*, the face frame rails and stiles are joined with mortises and tenons. A modern cabinetmaker would call this overkill; the joint is much stronger than what the assembly calls for. However, this is the way these frames were joined in days gone by, and David likes to remain as true to his furniture history as he can. However, if you aren't particularly attached to mortise-and-tenon joinery, you can easily substitute biscuits, dowels, or pocket screws.

Assemble the face frames, then glue them to the front edges of the cases. Take all necessary pains to make sure the openings in the face frames remain square.

INSTALLING THE TOP MOLDING

The top of the top case is topped off with a simple "sprung" molding — a flat board that leans out from the case at a 45 degree angle. To make the molding, double-bevel the edges of the molding stock as shown in the *Molding Joinery Detail*. Attach the horizontal soffit boards to the top of the case with wood screws, mitering the boards where they meet at the corners. Then attach the sprung moldings, driving flathead wood screws from inside the case or down through the soffits.

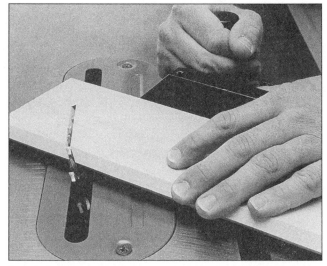

To join the sprung molding at the corners, you must *compound miter* the adjoining surfaces. That is, you must miter them with both the miter gauge and the blade set at an angle. Set the miter gauge to 54¾ degrees and the blade to 30 degrees. This is the proper setting for a molding that's sprung or sloped at 45 degrees. For different slopes, you must use different settings.

MAKING THE DOORS

The doors are frame-and-panel construction with the frame members joined with mortises and tenons. Each frame has a middle stile, and the inside edges of the members are cut with a decorative bead. The extra stiles and the beads add visual interest.

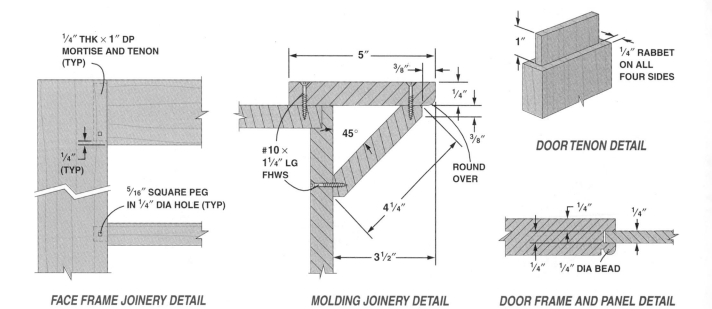

¼″ THK × 1″ DP MORTISE AND TENON (TYP)

¼″ (TYP)

⁵⁄₁₆″ SQUARE PEG IN ¼″ DIA HOLE (TYP)

FACE FRAME JOINERY DETAIL

5″

³⁄₈″

¼″

45°

#10 × 1¼″ LG FHWS

³⁄₈″

ROUND OVER

4¼″

3½″

MOLDING JOINERY DETAIL

1″

¼″ RABBET ON ALL FOUR SIDES

DOOR TENON DETAIL

¼″   ¼″

¼″   ¼″ DIA BEAD

DOOR FRAME AND PANEL DETAIL

JOINING THE DOOR FRAMES Cut grooves in the inside edges of the rails, outside stiles, and inside stiles, and in both edges of the middle stiles. These will hold the panels. Then cut or rout mortises in the outside stiles, inside stiles, and the center of the rails. Make matching tenons in the ends of the rails and middle stiles.

Next, cut beads in the outside faces of the same edges where you cut grooves. Using a band saw and a fence, trim away the bead from the area around the mortises and miter the beads on both the mortised and tenoned frame members. When you assemble the frames, the beads should meet at the miters.

Also cut ⅜-inch-wide, ⅜-inch-deep rabbets in the *outside* edges of the inside door stiles on the top and bottom doors, as shown in the *Inside Stile Detail*. These rabbets interlock when the doors are closed.

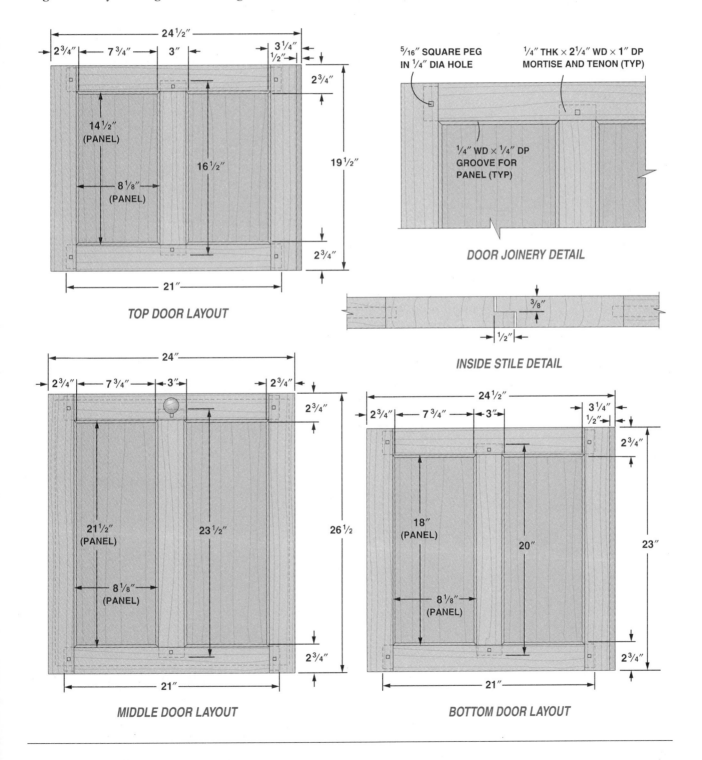

TOP DOOR LAYOUT

DOOR JOINERY DETAIL

INSIDE STILE DETAIL

MIDDLE DOOR LAYOUT

BOTTOM DOOR LAYOUT

METHODS OF WORK ■ *Joining Door Frames with Decorative Edges*

There are several ways to make paneled doors with decorative edges. You can buy special cutters to make a cope-and-stick joint on your table-mounted router or shaper. These are expensive, however, and unless you are making a lot of doors, they aren't worth the money or the time it takes to set them up.

You can also make small moldings and glue them to the inside edges of the frame members after the doors are assembled. This works well, but small moldings just ¼ inch wide are sometimes difficult to make.

The easiest method I've run across for short runs and single cabinets is to cut the decorative edge in the frame members, them miter the decorative portion.

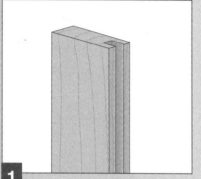

1 **Cut a groove** in the inside edges of the frame members to hold the door panel.

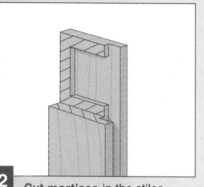

2 **Cut mortises** in the stiles, making them the same width as the grooves. You can rout the mortises, or drill a series of overlapping holes to remove most of the waste. Afterward, square the corners and clean up the sides with a chisel.

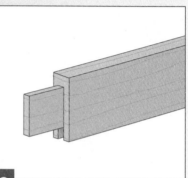

3 **Cut matching tenons** in the ends of the stiles. The inside surface of the tenon should be flush with the bottom of the groove.

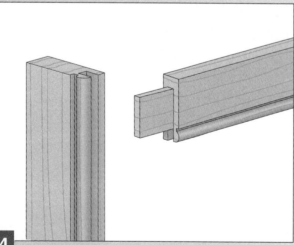

4 **Cut decorative shapes** on the outside surfaces of the grooved edges. These shapes must be no wider than the grooves are deep.

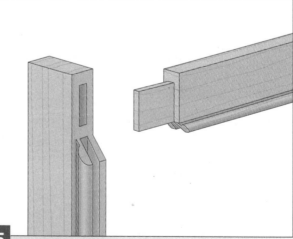

5 **Cut away both** the shaped and unshaped sides of the grooves from the frame members on both sides of the mortises. Where the mortise is near the end of a board, pare away the groove sides all the way to the end. Miter the groove sides at 45 degrees where they will meet when you assemble the mortise-and-tenon joints.

QUICK FIXTURE ■ *Frame-and-Panel Construction Aids*

MITER SHOOTING BLOCK

It's difficult to cut accurate miters in such small surfaces as the shaped sides of the grooves in the frame members. But this tiny jig helps you make dead-on accurate miters in the smallest surfaces.

Cut grooves in the bottom of the block the same size as the sides of the grooves in the frame members. The jig should fit loosely over the grooved edges. Adjust your table saw to make a 45 degree miter, and *test* the setup by making several cuts in scraps to make sure the setup is accurate. Then miter one end of the block.

To use the jig, fit it to the frame member where you want to make a miter. Using the mitered surface to guide a chisel, shave the wood to a 45 degree angle.

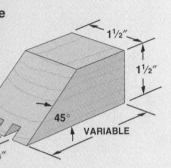

TENONING JIG

A tenoning jig holds boards vertically as you cut their ends. It's especially useful for making tenons in narrow boards.

Cut the parts of the jig and assemble them with glue, all except for the backstop. Instead, just screw this part into place. This lets you replace the backstop when it gets chewed up or when you need to hold the work at an angle.

To use the jig, rest the work against the backstop and clamp it to the face. This will keep it from shifting as it's cut. Guide the jig along a fence or straightedge as you work.

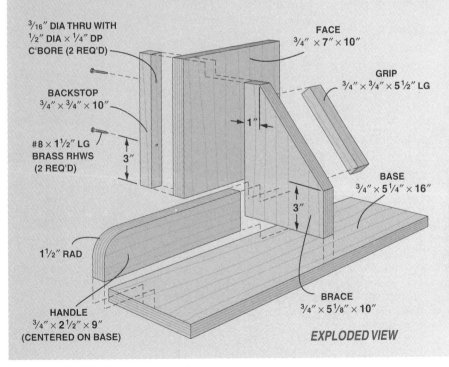

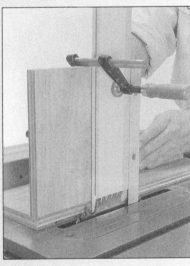

EXPLODED VIEW

METHODS OF WORK ■ *Driving Square Pegs in Round Holes*

David T. Smith pins his door mortise-and-tenon joints together by driving square pins or *pegs* through round holes, in the fashion of old-time country cabinetmakers. This time-proven method works much better than using round pegs or dowels. The square pegs wedge themselves in the holes and can't work loose.

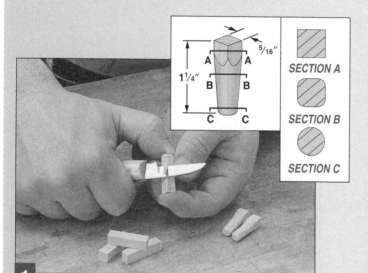

1 **Cut square stock for the pegs** from an extremely hard wood such as rock maple or hickory. Cut the pegs to a length you can comfortably grip and whittle about ¾ of its length, making it more and more round toward one end. When you've finished, it should be square on one end and round on the other, *but not tapered.*

2 **Assemble the mortise-and-tenon joint.** Drill a hole as big around as the peg is square completely through the parts that are to be pegged together. The hole should pass through both the mortise and the tenon.

3 **Coat the peg with glue** and drive it into the hole, round end first, with a mallet. Tap it so the top is almost (but not quite) flush with the surface of the wood. About ¹⁄₁₆ inch should protrude, and the square portion should be firmly wedged in the hole. Be careful not to hit the peg so hard it splinters. **Tip: If you have difficulty, try an epoxy glue. Water-based glues may cause the peg to swell.**

4 **Cut the rounded portion** protruding from the back of the assembly flush with the surface of the wood. Lightly sand the front surface, rounding over the peg slightly — this imitates the look of pegs in old pieces. Or, if you prefer, sand it flush.

ASSEMBLING THE DOORS Prefinish the door panels. Glue the door frames together, sliding the panels into their grooves as you do so. *Don't* glue the panels, however. They should "float" in the grooves, free to expand and contract.

INSTALLING WRITING SURFACES The middle doors are actually drop-down desk tops. As such, the back sides require a smooth work surface. First, fit the doors to their opening, sanding or planing them to their final size. Cut pieces of ¼-inch plywood just 1½ inches narrower and shorter than the middle doors. Cover these pieces with leather or a leather-like vinyl. (I recommend the vinyl. It looks as good as leather for this application, it wears better, and it produces a smoother writing surface.) Adhere the material with contact cement, wrapping it around the edges, then screw the pencil ledge to the surface. Fasten the work surface to the inside surfaces of the middle doors with ovalhead screws and finishing washers.

HANGING THE DOORS Install the doorstop strips in the top cabinet. Mark the positions of the hinges on the face frame. Note that the middle doors are hinged at the *bottom,* so they will drop down. The doors rest against the front edge of the counter, which holds them at a slight angle from horizontal. Fit the remaining doors to their openings, then wedge them in place. There should be a ¹⁄₁₆-inch gap between the doors and the face frames on all sides.

Transfer the hinge marks from the face frame to the door frames. Then remove the doors and cut mortises for butt hinges. Attach the hinges first to the doors, then attach the doors to the face frames. Also install pulls and catches.

MAKING THE PIGEONHOLES

The pigeonholes are a small shelving unit that fits in the right side of the top cabinet, between the divider and the false side. The arrangement shown in the *Pigeonhole Insert* drawings is only a suggestion; you can change the configuration to suit your own needs.

Before you settle on a design, measure the space where you will install the insert. If the dimensions have changed from your original plans, alter the dimensions of the pigeonhole to compensate. (Actually, you should make the insert about ⅛ inch *smaller* than the space so you don't have to force the insert when you install it.)

Cut parts to size, then cut the dadoes and rabbets needed. Glue the pieces together, checking that the assembly is square. After the glue dries, rest the pigeonholes inside the top cabinet, against the back. You may fasten them in place by driving flathead wood screws through the sides and into the case parts, or simply let them rest there.

> **Look Here! For more information on sizing pigeonholes, see page 50.**

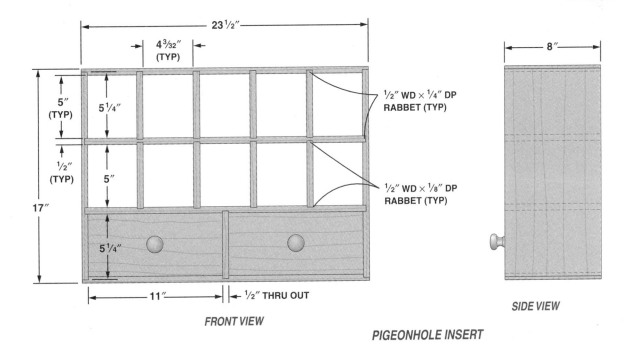

FRONT VIEW

SIDE VIEW

PIGEONHOLE INSERT

MAKING THE DRAWERS AND SHELVES

There are three types of drawers in the computer secretary desk, as it's designed — file drawers, sliding shelves (which are made like shallow drawers), and pigeonhole drawers. Each is made slightly differently.

MAKING THE SLIDING SHELVES The sliding shelves are just simple boxes. The front and back join the sides with half-blind dovetails, and the bottom rests in grooves. If you don't want the grooves to show on the assembled shelves, cut stopped grooves in the fronts and backs.

> **Look Here! For more information on routing half-blind dovetails, see page 62.**

MAKING THE FILE DRAWERS Like the sliding shelves, the file drawers are simple boxes, joined by half-blind dovetails and grooves. These drawers, however, have tall faces applied to the fronts.

The file drawers are sized to accommodate frames for hanging files. If you don't use these frames, you have to make the backs of the drawers as high as the faces.

CONSIDER THIS

The sliding shelves are intended to hold computer peripherals such as printers and scanners. This equipment all has sockets for plugs and cables, on/off switches, and other controls that must remain easily accessible. As designed, the sides of the sliding shelves may interfere with these features. Look over your equipment *before* you build the shelves — you may need to cut recesses in the front, back, or sides.

HANGING THE SLIDING SHELVES AND FILE DRAWERS Both the sliding shelves and the file drawers travel on full extension slides, allowing you to reach all the way to the back of each assembly. To hang the drawers, first remove the mounts from the slides. Fasten the mounts to the sides of the shelves and drawers, and the slides to the support frames and dividers.

> **Look Here! For more information on hanging drawers on extension slides, see page 63.**

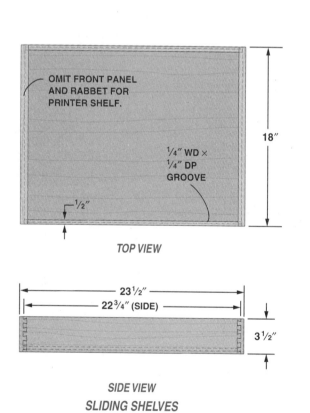

OMIT FRONT PANEL AND RABBET FOR PRINTER SHELF.

1/4" WD × 1/4" DP GROOVE

18"

1/2"

TOP VIEW

23 1/2"
22 3/4" (SIDE)

3 1/2"

SIDE VIEW
SLIDING SHELVES

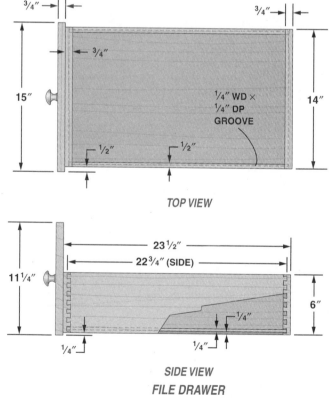

3/4"   3/4"

3/4"

15"   1/4" WD × 1/4" DP GROOVE   14"

1/2"   1/2"

TOP VIEW

23 1/2"
22 3/4" (SIDE)

11 1/4"   1/4"

6"

1/4"   1/4"

SIDE VIEW
FILE DRAWER

Make sure each pair of slides is perfectly parallel and at exactly the same height, otherwise the shelves and drawers will bind. Snap the mounts into the slides and test the action.

MAKING THE PIGEONHOLE DRAWERS The pigeonhole drawers are made in a more traditional manner. In each one the front joins the sides with half-blind dovetails, and the back rests in dadoes in the sides. The bottom slides into grooves in the sides and the front and is fastened to the back.

If you use a router and a jig to make the half-blind dovetails, note that the drawer fronts and sides are two different thicknesses. Most fixtures are designed to create dovetails in parts that are ¾ inch thick. However, if your jig isn't adjustable, you can compensate with spacers.

Using double-faced carpet tape, attach a scrap of ¼-inch-thick wood or plywood to the outside surface of the drawer sides before mounting them in the jig. (The spacer should face away from you when mounted.) Also attach a ¼-inch spacer to the end of the drawer front. When the front is mounted in the jig, the spacer will shift the end ¼ inch back from its usual position. Rout the dovetails, cutting through both spacers.

Assemble the drawer front, sides, and back with glue and let it dry. Then slide the drawer bottoms into their grooves. Fasten the bottoms to the backs with brads, driving the brads up through the bottoms and into the edge of the sides.

To install the drawers, sand or plane the outside surfaces, making each drawer slightly smaller than its opening. Test the fit — it should slide in and out of the pigeonhole assembly without binding.

FINISHING THE DESK

This is a big piece and it's going to take a prodigious amount of finish work; there's no two ways about it. But you can lighten the load quite a bit by sanding and scraping as you go. That is, as you build a component or subassembly, finish sand it, all accept for the very last grit. When you get to this stage, all you'll have left to do is a little touch-up sanding and a once-over with the last grit.

Why wait to sand with the last grit? There are two reasons. First, it's wise to wet a surface down with a damp cloth and give it a final sanding before you apply a finish. The light wetting makes the "whiskers" — loose wood fibers — stand up so you can knock them off with the sandpaper. If you go ahead and apply a finish, they will become imbedded in the finish and this will detract from the appearance of the piece. Wet the surface, let it dry completely, then sand with the last grit.

Second, a wood surface, when it's first exposed to the air, begins to *case harden*. In just a few days time, it's much less permeable than it was when you first exposed it. Consequently, it will not absorb a stain or a finish as well as it might immediately after sanding. The final sanding removes the hardened shell and renews the surface. Apply the finish as soon after the final sanding as possible; don't wait or the surface will harden again.

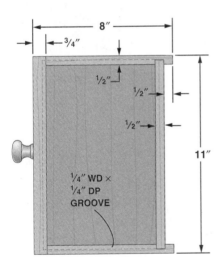

TOP VIEW

SIDE VIEW
PIGEONHOLE DRAWER

Workshop Secretary

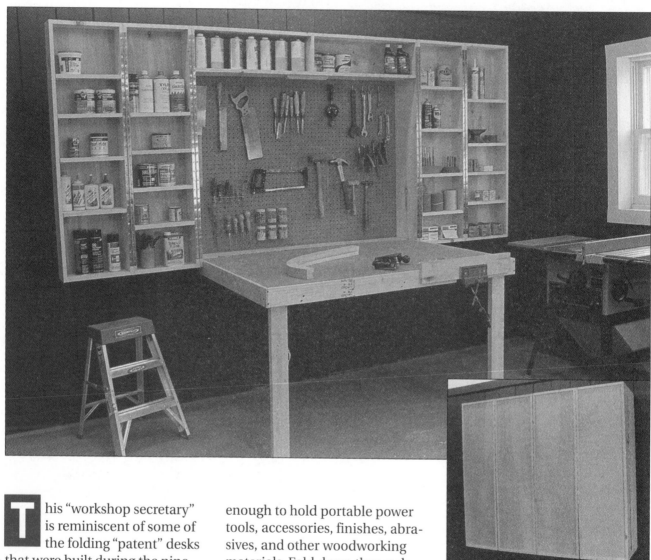

This "workshop secretary" is reminiscent of some of the folding "patent" desks that were built during the nineteenth century, particularly those by the Wooton Desk Company. When unfolded, these were massive office desks with cabinets on either side, offering shelves, cupboards, drawers, and pigeonholes galore. But they folded up into a neat little cabinet about the size of a large-screen television.

This piece of workshop furniture does much the same thing. Open the doors, and they become shelving units deep enough to hold portable power tools, accessories, finishes, abrasives, and other woodworking materials. Fold down the work surface and you have an area large enough to build projects of any size or complexity. Behind it, there's a broad expanse of pegboard to hold frequently used hand tools. And this all folds up, out of the way when you're not using it. It's perfect for craftsmen who share their shop with the family car, or who occasionally need an extra bench for assembly and finishing.

Features

15 square feet of hanging storage

30 running feet of shelving space

Large, rigid work surface

Built-in vise

Hangs on the wall

Folds up into a nest box just 4 feet by 5 feet

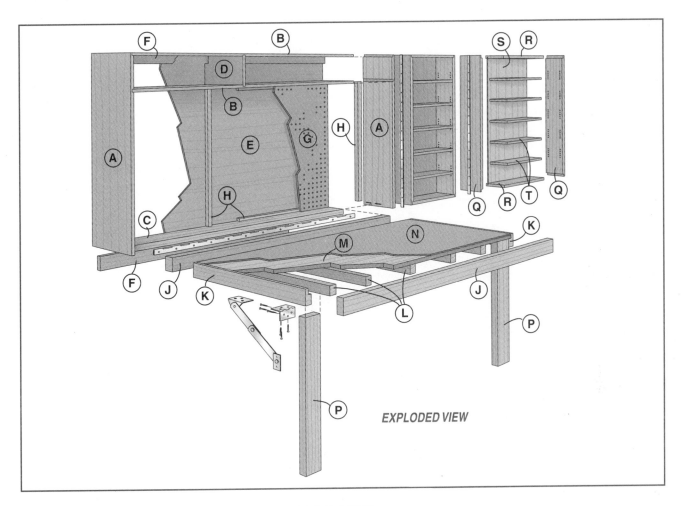

EXPLODED VIEW

WORKSHOP SECRETARY ■ *MATERIALS LIST* (Finished Dimensions)

PARTS — MAIN CABINET

A	Sides (2)	¾″ × 11″ × 47½″
B	Shelves (2)	¾″ × 10¾″ × 59¼″
C	Bottom shelf	1½″ × 7¼″ × 59¼″
D	Divider	¾″ × 10¾″ × 8⅞″
E	Back*	¼″ × 59¼″ × 47½″
F	Nailing strips (2)	¾″ × 3″ × 58½″
G	Pegboard	¼″ × 36⅜″ × 58½″
H	Cleats (total)	¾″ × ¾″ 230″

PARTS — WORK SURFACE

J	Front/back rails (2)	1½″ × 3½″ × 58¼″
K	Outside stiles (2)	1½″ × 3½″ 33⅜″
L	Ribs (5)	1½″ × 2½″ × 33⅜″
M	Work surface core*	¾″ × 34⅞″ × 56¾″
N	Work surface‡	¼″ × 34⅞″ × 56¾″
P	Legs (2)	1½″ × 3½″ × 33⅛″

PARTS — SIDE CABINETS

Q	Sides (8)	¾″ × 5½″ × 47½″
R	Tops/bottoms (8)	¾″ × 5½″ × 14¼″
S	Backs* (4)	¼″ × 14¼″ × 46¾″
T	Adjustable shelves (20)	¾″ × 5″ × 13⅜″

* Make these parts from plywood.
‡ Make this part from tempered hardboard.

HARDWARE

1½″ × 48″ Piano hinges and mounting screws (5)
3½″ × 3½″ Butt hinges and mounting screws (2)
Heavy-duty folding leg braces and mounting screws (2)
#8 × 2½″ Construction screws (30)
#6 × 1⅝″ Construction screws (70)
Shelving support pins (80)
⅜″ × 4″ Lag screws with flat washers (6-8 sets)
#6 × 1¼″ Flathead wood screws (192)
#6 × ¾″ Flathead wood screws (14)

How do I build it?

Dan Garber of Dan's Wood Shop, Clayton, Ohio, collaborated with Marvin Olinsky and Joe McIntyre, proprietors of the Corn Crib in Dayton, Ohio, to build this bench as a collection of boxes. The largest box, of course, is the main cabinet. The side cabinets are just four boxes hinged to the main. Even the work surface could be considered a large, shallow box with reinforcing ribs.

PREPARING THE STOCK

The secretary is designed to be built from construction lumber (1-by and 2-by stock) and plywood. Because of this, you'll need to take some time to "shop dry" the lumber for several weeks. Dimensional lumber isn't dried to the same degree as cabinet grades. If you work the wood immediately, it will shrink considerably as you build the project.

After the wood has dried, cut all the parts to the sizes shown in the Materials List.

CUTTING THE JOINERY

To keep the secretary as simple as possible to build, Dan, Marvin, and Joe made as few joints as possible. All you have to cut are a few rabbets and dadoes:

■ ¾-inch-wide, ⅜-inch-deep dadoes in the main cabinet sides to hold the middle shelf

■ ¾-inch-wide, ⅜-inch-deep dadoes in the main cabinet shelves to hold the divider

■ ¾-inch-wide, ⅜-inch-deep rabbets in the two ends of the main cabinet sides to hold the top shelf

■ ¾-inch-wide, ⅜-inch-deep end rabbets in the side cabinet sides to hold the tops and bottoms

■ ¾-inch-wide, 1-inch-deep edge rabbets in the outside stiles to hold the work surface

■ ¼-inch-wide, ⅜-inch-deep edge rabbets in the main cabinet sides to hold the back

■ ¼-inch-wide, ⅜-inch-deep grooves in the side cabinet tops, bottoms, and sides to hold the backs

■ Biscuit joints in the ends of the bottom shelf and the inside faces of the main cabinet sides. If you don't have a biscuit cutter, you may also use ¼-inch-thick plywood splines.

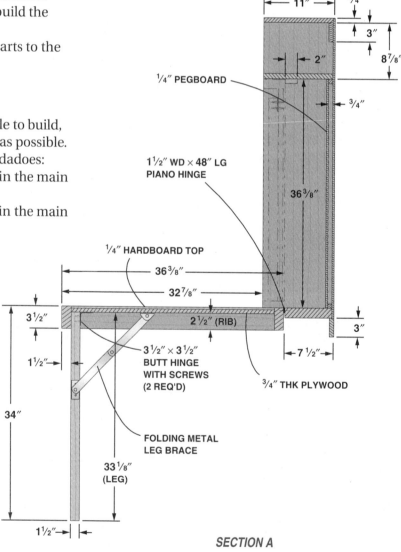

SECTION A

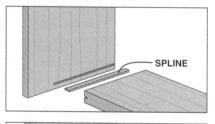

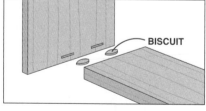

SHELF-TO-SIDE JOINT

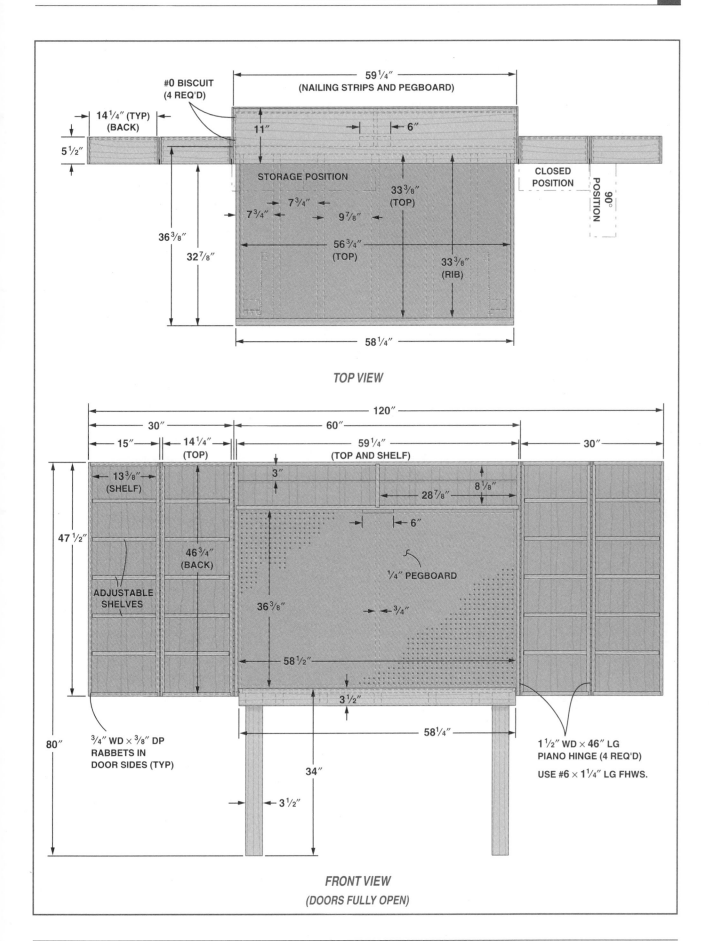

TOP VIEW

FRONT VIEW

(DOORS FULLY OPEN)

The dadoes and rabbets in the shelves and sides can be made with a router or a dado cutter. You may find it easier, however, to cut the deep rabbets in the stiles on a table saw. Make each rabbet in two passes, first ripping a ¾-inch-deep kerf in the face of the stock, then a 1-inch-deep kerf in the edge to free the waste.

DRILLING THE SUPPORT HOLES

The adjustable shelves in the side cabinets rest on shelving support pins. These pins are inserted in rows of ¼-inch-diameter, ½-inch-deep holes in the sides, as shown in the *Side Cabinet Side Detail*. For the shelves to rest solidly on the pins, you must drill each row of holes precisely the same. To help do this, make the *Drilling Guide* shown.

When drilling the cabinet sides, insert the cleat on the edge of the guide in the ¼-inch-wide groove for the cabinet back. Drill one row of holes, then flip the guide edge for edge and hook the cleat over the front edge of the cabinet side. Drill the second set. To make sure both sets are aligned vertically, hook the cleat at the *top* of the guide over the shoulder of the top rabbet.

SAFEGUARD

When cutting a rabbet with a saw blade, make sure the waste is on the *outside* of the saw blade (the side opposite the fence) on the last pass. If the waste is on the inside, it may be pinched between the fence and the blade. This will cause it to kick back at you like a spear.

ASSEMBLING THE CABINETS

By and large, the secretary is assembled with glue and reinforced with screws. The screws not only add some strength to each joint, they also provide clamping pressure while the glue dries.

ASSEMBLING THE MAIN CABINET To assemble the main cabinet, glue the top shelf, middle shelf, and divider together, reinforcing the glue joints with construction screws. **Note: If you want to hide the heads of the screws, countersink *and* counterbore the screw holes, then cover the heads with wooden plugs. Sand the wooden plugs flush with the wood surface.**

Glue the sides to the top/middle shelf assembly and the bottom shelf. Reinforce the joints — including the biscuit joints between the bottom shelf and the sides — with screws.

5½"
¼"
1¼"
5⅜"
¼" DIA × ½" DP HOLE (TYP)
1" (TYP)
3¾" (TYP)
¼" WD × ⅜" DP GROOVE
47½"
¾"
¾" WD × ⅜" DP RABBET (TYP)

SIDE CABINET SIDE DETAIL

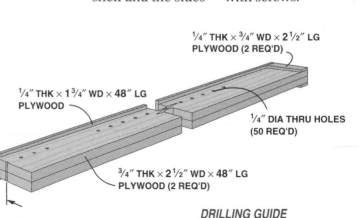

¼" THK × ¾" WD × 2½" LG PLYWOOD (2 REQ'D)
¼" THK × 1¾" WD × 48" LG PLYWOOD
¼" DIA THRU HOLES (50 REQ'D)
¾" THK × 2½" WD × 48" LG PLYWOOD (2 REQ'D)
¾"

DRILLING GUIDE

Attach the nailing strip to the assembly with glue and screws. Make sure the cabinet is square, then fasten the back in place with finishing nails.

Glue the vertical cleats to the back, one against the right cabinet side, another against the left, and the third in the middle. Add horizontal cleats top and bottom. Then attach the pegboard to the cleats with wood screws. The cleats keep the pegboard spaced ¾ inch away from the back. If you didn't have this space, you wouldn't be able to insert the hooks and other hardware needed for hanging tools on the pegboard.

Attach the stop to the underside of the middle shelf with glue and screws. The front edge of the stop must be 3½ inches from the front edge of the shelf.

ASSEMBLING THE SIDE CABINETS To assemble the side cabinets, glue the sides to the top and bottom, reinforcing the joints with screws. As you work, glue the backs in place in their grooves. Usually, you wouldn't glue the backs in place; you'd let them "float" in the grooves. But in this case, it's necessary to add strength and help keep the cabinets square.

ASSEMBLING THE WORK SURFACE Fasten the rails and stiles together with #8 × 2½-inch construction screws. Glue the core to the frame so it rests in the rabbets on the outside stiles. Then fasten the hardboard work surface to the core with flathead wood screws. *Don't* glue the work surface in place; just fasten it with screws. This allows you to replace the work surface from time to time as it becomes worn.

Fasten the legs to the bottom side of the core with butt hinges, then attach folding leg braces to keep the legs vertical.

JOINING THE CABINETS AND THE WORK SURFACE Lay the main cabinet flat on your workshop floor face up and arrange the side cabinets next to it. There should be two side cabinets to the left of the main cabinet and another two to the right. Using a hacksaw, trim the 48-inch-long piano hinges to 46 inches long, then attach them to the front edges of the cabinet sides, joining all five cabinets.

Attach one leaf of a piano hinge to the top of the work surface at the back edge. With a helper, stand the work surface up on the main cabinet so the top is flush with the top face of the bottom shelf. Attach the other leaf of the piano hinge to the bottom shelf.

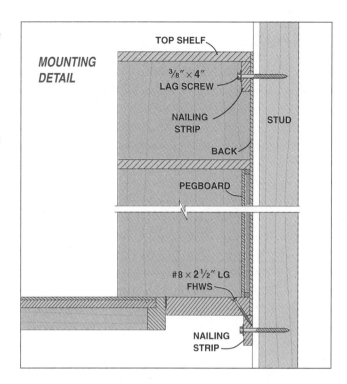

MOUNTING DETAIL

TOP SHELF
⅜" × 4" LAG SCREW
NAILING STRIP
STUD
BACK
PEGBOARD
#8 × 2½" LG FHWS
NAILING STRIP

Test the folding action. Fold the leg up under the work surface, then fold the work surface into the main cabinet. Finally, fold the side cabinets over the work surface.

Note: Dan, Marvin, and Joe clamped the jaws of the vise to the middle shelf to hold the work surface in the up position. If you don't have a vise, drill a ⅜-inch-diameter hole through the top shelf and into the work surface frame. Drop a 5/16-inch-diameter, 3-inch-long hex bolt through the hole to serve as a locking pin.

HANGING THE SECRETARY

To hang the secretary, detach one leaf of each piano hinge to separate the cabinets and the work surface.

Find the studs in your workshop wall. Or, if your shop is made from concrete block or masonry, install lead anchors in the wall where you want to attach the nailing strips. Mount the bottom nailing strip to the wall so the top edge is 32½ inches above the floor. Secure it to the studs or the lead anchors with lag screws.

With a helper, rest the main cabinet on the bottom nailing strip. Fasten the top nailing strip to the studs or anchors with lag screws, then shoot construction screws at an angle through the bottom shelf and into the bottom nailing strip. Reattach the side cabinets and the work surface to the main cabinet.

Index

B

Bookcases
  built-in, 3, 4, 24–41
  case, assembling, 15, 32, 33, 39
  case, joinery, 13, 31, 32
  case, making, 13, 15, 31
  case, squaring, 33
  corner unit, 26
  dimensions, 4, 5, 26
  doors, cupboard, 6, 34
  doors, fitting, 34, 35
  doors, hanging, 34, 35
  doors, installing, 19
  face frames, making and installing,
    16, 32, 38, 39
  hanging, 3, 19
  leveling, 39
  materials, preparing, 11–13, 30
  shelves, adjustable, 6, 15, 19, 38
  shelves, sliding, 32, 36
  shelving, construction, 6
  shelving, support holes, drilling,
    15, 37
  standing, 3, 4
  styles, 7–9, 27
Book slip, 22, 23

D

Desk
  computer workstation, 52, 54, 55
  construction, 52–55
  secretary, 51–53
  writing, 52, 86
Desk, computer secretary
  cabinets, assembling, 107
  cases, making, 103, 108
  doors, hanging, 113
  doors, making, 108–113
  face frame, making and installing,
    108
  file drawers, making, 114
  materials, preparing, 103
  pigeonholes, making, 113–115
  shelves, sliding, 114
  size and styles, 97–99
Desk, pedestal
  case, assembling, 59, 60
  case, making, 57, 58
  computer cabinet, 64, 65
  construction, 52, 53, 55
  drawers, hanging, 63, 70, 71
  drawers, making, 61, 62, 69
  face frame, making, 59
  file cabinet, 49, 50, 57, 60, 61, 67, 69
  frame-and-panel construction, 57,
    58
  materials, preparing, 57, 67
  pedestals, building, 57–60
  size, 49, 50
  top, 67–69
  ventilation holes, 64
Desk, portable
  assembling, 95

box, joinery, 91–93
  materials, preparing, 89
  size and styles, 85–87
Desk, rolltop
  materials, preparing, 73
  pigeonholes, making and
    installing, 50, 80–83
  rolltop, installing, 83
  rolltop, making, 73–80
  styles, 51
  tambours, 49, 73, 76–79
Doors
  construction, 34
  cupboard, 34
  fitting, 34, 35
  frame, joinery, 17, 20, 21, 108–112
  frame-and-panel construction, 20,
    21, 34, 108–113
  glass and glazed, 3, 6, 17–20
  hanging, 19, 34, 35, 83, 113
  hinges, 19, 34, 35
  making, 17, 35, 108–113
  muntins, installing, 18
  tamboured, 73, 76–79
Drawers
  brackets, 70
  designing, 60, 61
  extension slides, 61, 63, 70, 71, 103,
    114, 115
  guides, 63
  hanging, 63, 70, 71
  joinery, 36, 62, 82
  making, 49, 60–63, 69, 108–114
  pigeonhole, 73, 81–83, 114, 115
  raised panel, making, 62

F

Filing cabinet
  drawers, making, 49, 60–63, 114
  size, 49, 50, 57, 60
  top, 67, 69
Finishing, 19, 22, 41, 46, 83, 95, 115

H

Hardware
  extension slides, 32, 36, 61, 63, 70,
    71, 103, 114, 115
  hinges, types, 34
  shelving supports, 38

J

Jigs and fixtures
  corner square, 33, 107
  drilling guide, 15, 37, 106, 120
  extension slide drill guide, 71
  fence extension and guide strip, 62
  finger joint jig, 92, 93
  miter shooting block, 111
  self-clamping guide, 13, 14, 46
  tambour assembly jig, 79
  tenoning jig, 20, 36, 111
Joinery
  biscuit joint, 16, 46, 106, 118
  breadboard, 89
  bridle joint, 20
  case, 13, 31, 103
  cope-and-stick joint, 21, 110

cope joint, 41
  corner lap joint, 17, 20
  dado, routing, 13, 46
  door, 17, 20, 21, 34, 108–113
  dovetails, routing, 23, 62
  dowel joint, making, 16, 31, 38
  drawer, 36, 62, 82
  face frame, 16, 31, 108
  finger joint, 91–93
  frame-and-panel construction, 20,
    21, 34, 57, 58, 108–113
  lock joint, making, 36, 82
  miter joint, cutting, 41, 111
  mortise-and-tenon, 18, 20, 21, 74,
    108, 110, 112
  nailing strip joinery, 31
  plywood joinery, cutting, 31
  round pegs in square holes, 112
  shelves, 36, 118

P

Pigeonholes, making and installing,
  50, 73, 80–83, 113–115

S

Shelves
  adjustable, 6, 15, 19, 38, 55, 120
  banding, 19
  dimensions, 4, 5, 26
  extension slides, 32, 36, 103, 114,
    115
  inset, 42, 43
  joinery, 36, 118
  quick-and-easy, 44–47
  shelving, construction, 6
  shelving, support holes, drilling,
    15, 37, 106, 120
  shelving, supports, 38
  sliding, 32, 36, 114, 115
  support pins, 37, 38, 120
Skills
  banding a plywood edge, 67
  designing and assembling tam-
    boured doors, 78,79
  driving round pegs in square holes,
    112
  finding studs, 39
  installing corner molding, 41
  joining breadboard ends, 89
  joining door frames with decora-
    tive edges, 110
  laying out an oval, 73
  making a dowel joint, 38
  making a lock joint, 36, 82
  making cove molding, 16
  making finger joints, 93
  routing half-blind dovetails, 62
  squaring a case, 33
  truing a board, 11

W

Wood
  busting down, 11
  double-cutting sheet materials, 30
  shop drying, 11
Workshop secretary, 116–121

A few essential woodworking secrets...

Dress for success.

- Always wear eye protection — safety glasses for most operations, a full face shield for turning, routing, and other operations that throw wood chips. Always presume that every board you cut has a splinter with your name on it.

- Wear a dust mask when sanding and sawing — sawdust (especially fine sawdust) may be harmful to your lungs.

- Wear hearing protectors when routing or planing and for long, continuous power-tool operations. The high frequencies can harm your ears.

- Wear rubber gloves when handling dangerous chemicals — many of these can harm your skin or can be absorbed through the skin.

- Wear a vapor mask when finishing — the vapors of some finishing chemicals are potentially toxic.

- Wear close-fitting clothes with the sleeves rolled up above the elbows. Remove jewelry or anything that might catch on a tool.

Work smart.

- Install good lighting — it helps to see what you're doing.

- Hang or store tools within easy reach — the work goes faster.

- Keep your work area free of clutter — you don't want to trip when surrounded by sharp tools.

- Install a circuit breaker box within easy reach, and make sure each circuit is grounded and rated for sufficient amperage.

- Keep blades and cutters sharp and free of pitch — a dull tool is harder to control and therefore more dangerous than a sharp one.

- Keep arbors, tables, and fences properly aligned — misaligned tools are an accident waiting to happen.

- Keep tables and fences waxed and rust-free — this gives you more control over your work.

- Store flammable chemicals in fireproof containers. The same goes for shop rags. Some finishes generate heat as they cure and may cause rags to combust spontaneously.

Work safe.

- Keep the blade and cutter guards in place. They're like seat belts — they're a bother at first, but pretty soon you will feel uncomfortable without them.

- Mark the danger zones around blades and cutters, and keep your hands and fingers out of these areas.